8 Steps to Building
Innovating Organizations

8 Steps to Building Innovating Organizations

Manu Parashar

Response Books
A Division of Sage Publications
New Delhi/Thousand Oaks/London

Copyright © Manu Parashar, 2007

First published in 2007 by

Response Books
A division of Sage Publications India Pvt Ltd
B 1/I 1, Mohan Cooperative Industrial Area
Mathura Road, New Delhi 110 044

Sage Publications Inc	**Sage Publications Ltd**
2455 Teller Road	1 Oliver's Yard
Thousand Oaks	55 City Road
California 91320	London EC1Y 1SP

Published by Vivek Mehra for Response Books, Laser typeset in 11/13 points Sabon by Excellent Laser Typesetters, Delhi, and printed at Chaman Enterprises, New Delhi.

Library of Congress Cataloging-in-Publication Data

Parashar, Manu, 1971–
    8 steps to building innovating organizations/Manu Parashar.
        p. cm.
    Includes bibliographical references and index.

1. Knowledge management. 2. Business enterprises—Technological innovations. 3. Creative ability in business. 4. Technological innovations—Management. I. Title. II. Title: Eight steps to building innovating organizations.

HD30.2.P369	658.4'063—dc22	2007	2006034193

ISBN: 10: 0–7619–3559–2 (PB)   10: 81–7829–718–3 (India-PB)
          13: 978–0–7619–3559–9 (PB) 13: 978–81–7829–718–7 (India-PB)

Production Team: Swati Sahi, Mathew and Santosh Rawat

Contents

❀

Contents

List of Tables

❀

List of Figures

❉

Foreword

❋

Innovation is key to the survival and growth of any organization. Since the opening of the economy in the early 1990s, most Indian organizations, old and new, have recognized the importance of innovation for their long-term performance. More recently, several large Indian companies have developed global ambitions that are predicated on innovation. However, many of these same organizations have not achieved much success in translating their desire for innovation into concrete tangible outcomes. This may be largely attributed to the inability of their leaders to fully appreciate the innovation process and to create organizational capabilities that support the process as it translates a creative idea/invention into a commercially viable innovation.

The process of innovation in an organization is quite complex. First, contrary to popular perception, an innovation is not a product of an inspired thought of a genius. Thomas Edison, who is often portrayed as one of those geniuses, had noted that inventive genius is "99% perspiration and 1% inspiration". Second, successful innovation requires the involvement and support of a large number of very talented people—it is a team effort. A typical innovation is the output of a multidisciplinary team working together over a long period of time, and interacting with many experts outside the team and in the market. Third, not all inventions or innovations are a result of processes that deliver outcomes as planned. Chance plays a big role in throwing up new ideas and opportunities for their application. And finally, it is a well-accepted truth that inventions that lead to successful innovations often result from random accidents or experiments that went awry. The capabilities that are required to support such an understanding of the innovation process are very different from those that are required for the normal activities in an organization.

This book does an excellent job of explaining in a very lucid manner the nuances of the innovation process. More importantly, it presents a set of guidelines that will allow business leaders interested in innovation to build the necessary capabilities in their organizations to support the innovation process every step of the journey. Manu Parashar has included concepts from the most current literature on innovation in a very reader-friendly language. He has sprinkled very fascinating examples and case studies from well-known firms in India and abroad to illustrate the application of these concepts in practice. He has also revealed his personal insights from his involvement with the innovation process in a few organizations.

I believe that this book will be beneficial to anyone who is passionate about innovation, and is interested in transforming his or her organization into one that is innovation capable.

Abhoy K. Ojha   July 2006
Professor
Organizational Behaviour and
Human Resource Management
Indian Institute of Management Bangalore
Bangalore

Acknowledgements

❄

निंदक नेड़ा राखिए आँगन कुटी बंधाइ।
बिना सांबण पांणी बिना, निरमल करे सुभाइ।।

Kabir

Keep your critic close. Build him a home in your courtyard.
Without soap, without water, he would keep your attitude pure.

I have been fortunate enough to be surrounded by
people who provide me with constructive criticism. To
their credit my often violent reactions have not deterred
anyone. I owe this book, and possibly my pure attitude to my critics. May they grow from strength to
strength and take me with them.

Manu Parashar   July 2006
Bangalore

Introduction

❋

Business has always been about ideas that can generate a profit. These ideas are what get a business started, help it survive, grow, and contribute to society. All businesses start with a seed idea that gives them an opportunity to provide value to their customers and they earn a part of this value generated as profit. Their continued growth and successes depends on coming up with new ideas to serve their customers better. These ideas represent innovation. Innovation is the soul and spirit of a successful organization. Innovation can take place in every sphere; in products, in distribution, in administrative processes, in logistics. The list is endless. And so are the possibilities.

The 21st century has also resulted in a world that not only seems speeded up but also significantly smaller and crowded. The rate of change today is blinding. Technologies are launched and become obsolete in a flash. Product life-cycles are being reduced to miniscule proportions. Even the process life-cycles are smaller, and a process implementation provides only a fleeting advantage. The only way to stay competitive is to stay well ahead of the change curve.

The other aspect of 21st century change is that globalization, information technology, internet, and improved transportation infrastructure have actually made the world a smaller place. Change or innovation travels across the world at lightning speed. The reaction time to change is almost infinitesimal. This also ensures that best practices or innovations are copied much quicker and therefore the advantage they give is temporary. Thomas Friedman and Nandan Nilekani call this "the flattening of the world".

In this flattening process, organizations can no longer rely on an unequal distribution of knowledge to give them a long term competitive advantage. They need to stay either at or close to the leading edge of change to take advantage of this ever changing environment. This can happen only by creating new knowledge or innovating continuously. Creating an ever flowing stream of innovations is no longer a luxury but a necessity.

In recent times, businesses the world over have been challenged by the marketplace. Some have been defeated by financial and ethical issues, such as Kmart, or others closer to home, Hindustan Motors or Fiat India have simply been unable to cope. Across the business landscape there are lesser stories, stories of companies who are simply drifting their way to the future; whose innovations are serendipitous rather than planned. These are the companies that do well but never well enough.

One thing is common to these companies—their view on innovation. The traditional view of innovation was restricted to the research & development department, or perhaps the marketing department. The activity was episodic, as part of a larger picture of new product planning or of product refreshment. In today's world, that is no longer possible. Somewhere, somehow, some competitor is going to come up to you and say, "Smile, you're on Candid Camera!"— and your new product becomes a joke.

Organizations need a continuous stream of novel profitable ideas that gives them a sustainable competitive edge. The ability of an organization to gear its processes towards innovation and deliver novel profitable ideas is its innovation capability.

In this book, the focus is on showing organizations how the capability to innovate can be systematically built into the fabric of the organization. The components of knowledge, attitude and creativity are discussed. Throughout the book, the model is illustrated with examples from great innovative organizations like IBM, Google, Dupont, Proctor & Gamble, ITC and Tata Motors. What makes these organizations special is their commitment to continuous and sustained innovation and the systematic way in which they achieve it. Their experiences in building innovative organizations serve as guide posts as well as inspiration, for the reader. Some of these organizations are over 100 years old, and still others have innovation practices dating to the early 1900s. They provide a mix of insights that are not just interesting but relevant, timeless, and applicable to a wide variety of organizations.

Just as the concept of travel is timeless but generations never tire of it, and people keep discovering newer and different ways of seeing the world, the concept of innovation is timeless but organizations need to continuously work at it to build long lasting capabilities and keep themselves alive. Innovation can be a source of great competitive advantage that is not just ephemeral but can also give them strength to survive and flourish. The hope is that this book may just be the first small step for many organizations on that journey.

One aspect of innovation capability as you will discover in the coming pages is the merit of using knowledge from diverse sources. You may recognize some of them and some of them may be new to you. At the end of the matter, if the reader can get new knowledge out of this book, then the task is done.

1 | What is Innovation?

One of the single biggest innovations to shape our world has been the printing press. It took civilization from the realm of handwritten books that took priests 20 years to write to printed paperbacks that are sold for Rs 50 on the footpaths. And one man was largely responsible for that shift. Johannes Gutenberg put together a printing press in 1440 that with refinements remained the process of choice for printing until as late as the 20th century.

Gutenberg's printing process was not entirely invented from scratch either. What Gutenberg actually did was use and combine different types of knowledge that he had seen or heard of over the years. He had probably seen examples of block printed Chinese playing cards or paper money in Europe and got the idea of movable block printing from them. Pi Sheng, in 1041, was the inventor of the Chinese process of clay typeset in frames, pressed on to paper. The Chinese script is so complex that 5,000 characters were needed to create a full-length book. However, the Roman script as we all know is far simpler. Gutenberg's experimentation with metal blocks in 1430 required him to develop only 26 characters.

Gutenberg was a goldsmith, a metal worker, but he also had the soul of an artist. He was not content with creating the movable metal type out of a complex process where he used steel rods to cast the type that were then impressed upon copper plates to create matrices to be used as moulds. He also wanted to imitate almost exactly the beautiful calligraphy of the books of the time. Gutenberg not only created the type with the perfectly regular spacing of calligraphic writing but he also made a typeset that captured cursive writing. His artistry was so unparalleled at the time that only four such cursive types are known to have existed in that era and all four were attributed to Gutenberg.

Not only did Gutenberg's process of the movable metal type enable the reproduction of books, it sparked off no less than a revolution in its related fields. Till that time, in Europe, books were made on vellum (which was lamb/calf skin) and the early printed books also used the same material. But as demand for books increased, paper technology had to make substantial advances to enable the printing of books on paper. Paper was also a Chinese invention, but the Gutenberg process created a demand for paper in Europe like that had never been seen before. Nor was ink technology far behind in advancement. The previous wood-cut method used water based inks or an egg based tempura. However, such inks would not remain on metal types and therefore, viscous oil based inks that had been developed around the 10th century were adapted by Gutenberg for the metal type process.

Finally, Gutenberg needed a press to put all of these together into a book. Previously, presses of a fashion were being used in wine and cheese making. Gutenberg adapted a similar thought into a printing press that enabled an operator to press the type on to paper and then lift it off leaving behind the impression.

This revolution took a continuous commitment on Gutenberg's part for more than 20 years and was an enormously expensive process. Beginning with his first prototypes in 1430, Gutenberg started building his press in 1436. His first examples of printing were papal indulgence slips in 1440, which were used to pardon sins of people who were rich enough to purchase them from the Church. The first mass produced Gutenberg Bibles began to appear in 1452 and by 1499, there were as many as 2,500 printing houses across Europe, and it was rumored that 15 million books had been published.

Gutenberg had created this revolution by combining a lot of disparate ideas together. And the unique combination of ideas that he came up with changed the world forever.

What is Innovation?
❋

The printing press is a truly breakthrough innovation, isn't it? What can be learnt from the Gutenberg story? The story is a veritable treasure trove as far as innovation is concerned. One of the first lessons is that innovation is all about combining various kinds of knowledge in a unique manner.[1] Gutenberg combined knowledge from fields that were very different from each other. All knowledge existed in one form or the other but only Gutenberg managed to combine calligraphy, ink technology, paper technology, metal working and mechanical engineering together. The result of this combination changed the world. In a sense, this example both illuminates innovation as a process and also illustrates what goes into innovation. The content of innovation is knowledge while the process is the combination of knowledge.

Different types of existing knowledge form the input and the combining of these types of knowledge leads to an output, which is new knowledge. The output of the innovation process itself hence is new knowledge. Creating this new knowledge is the process of innovation. Gutenberg created the field of printing technology, a field of knowledge that did not exist before.

New ideas, concepts, products, services, technology, etc. all represent new knowledge and are a result of a process of knowledge creation. This also means that any new combination of two or more kinds of knowledge can be construed as innovation. But is all innovation the same? No, of course not. We all instinctively know that some innovations transform our lives but others just merely improve or worsen it. The mobile phone is one such device that transformed lives. However, the polyphonic ring tone on mobile phones is only a peripheral source of entertainment or irritation, depending on whether you are its owner or its audience. Then what differentiates breakthrough innovations from incremental innovations?

Quantum Jumps vs Baby Steps

❀

Very simply, a breakthrough innovation is one that has the potential to further human knowledge and radically change the world. It is created when many different kinds of knowledge are combined. Not only are the knowledge bases different but they also have very little overlap. This combination of knowledge pushes the boundaries of knowledge far beyond existing ones. Take space travel, for instance. Try to figure out the number of different kinds of knowledge that are combined to create space travel. The list that you will end up with will be very long indeed. From fluid mechanics to human physiology; from organic chemistry to electronics, and so on. Breakthrough innovations need a combination of a large number of knowledge areas.

Essentially there are two dimensions that determine the extent to which an innovation can be classified as breakthrough or incremental (see Figure 1.1). The first dimension is the types of knowledge combined, varying from the small to large. If a large variety of knowledge is being combined then a breakthrough innovation may result. But of course, this is not the only factor. Also important is the extent of overlap in the knowledge being combined. A low degree of overlap in the types of knowledge being combined can result in a more radical innovation.

The two dimensions of the types of knowledge and the overlap in knowledge leads to the classification of innovation into four broad categories—Kaizen, incremental/efficiency, radical and breakthrough.

The Kaizen school of thought is meant to improve existing processes rather than achieve a specific goal. Kaizen has five founding elements—teamwork, personal discipline, improved morale, quality circles and suggestions for improvement. On this base, are constructed the three Kaizen pillars, efficiency, 5S and standardization. Kaizen creates small amounts of new knowledge by focusing on improving status quo and on employee commitment and discipline. Kaizen, therefore, is a very people-oriented concept. It usually does not take the organization very far in terms of radical

Figure 1.1: Types of Innovation

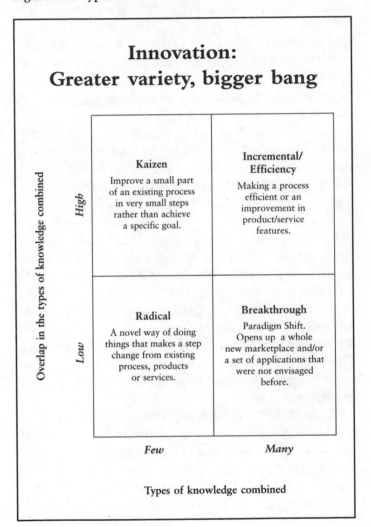

Innovation:
Greater variety, bigger bang

Overlap in the types of knowledge combined

High

Kaizen

Improve a small part
of an existing process
in very small steps
rather than achieve
a specific goal.

**Incremental/
Efficiency**

Making a process
efficient or an
improvement in
product/service
features.

Low

Radical

A novel way of doing
things that makes a step
change from existing
process, products
or services.

Breakthrough

Paradigm Shift.
Opens up a whole
new marketplace and/or
a set of applications that
were not envisaged
before.

Few   *Many*

Types of knowledge combined

or breakthrough innovation. But it does contribute to the overall competitiveness of the organization.

Incremental innovation usually results from the combination of many types of knowledge that have a high degree of overlap between them. This improves overall product and process but the impact created on target market is small. These changes do, however, add up over a period of time.

The Sony Walkman, when launched in 1979, created a stir across the world with its concept of personal music. Five years later, the Discman was launched. While technologically, the invention of the Discman was very different; in concept, the Discman was only incremental to that of the Walkman. Both played music from an external device that had limited memory. Every other difference was largely an incremental improvement—sound quality, memory space on the CD, handling ease. While many types of knowledge and technology were used in the creation of the Discman, the overlap between them and that of the Walkman was high. The philosophy of both devices is essentially the same. The Discman only represents incremental technology over the Walkman in a progressive time period.

Radical and breakthrough innovations radically change a product market and the lives of people it impacts. The launch of the Apple iPod was one such radical innovation. Apple took a portable music player, added a miniature hard disk and an OS and put it into the most beautiful design since the iMac—and created the iPod. The iPod has changed the face of portable music in our lives today. When compared to the Discman, the iPod was tiny, incredibly sleek, and it could hold between a 1,000 to 25,000 songs in a compressed MP3 format—compared to most standard music CDs that could hold only a few songs (usually in single digits). To top that, the users could create their own play-lists, manipulate the order in which the songs could be played and, in the latest video iPod version, watch the music video to go with it. As if all that was not enough, iPod also came with an internet service, iTunes, which enabled users to buy music online. The iPod outplayed the Discman on every front.

The reason it succeeded is because iPod combined very different kinds of knowledge. From sociological (looking good) to demographic (with rock star editions) to technical knowledge (massive memory and easy interface), a wide variety of knowledge has been combined in a unique manner. Because they draw from such wide sources, they create impact all around. Another brand that has created such impact is Crest. Crest, in 1955, was the first toothpaste that used fluoride. Until then toothpaste manufacturers had been unable to develop a way of mixing fluoride and the paste abrasive safely. P&G, with its research in detergents and hard water, knew quite a lot about minerals. Its researchers made the translation leap from detergents to toothpaste and developed the first toothpaste that had fluoride in it. Not only did P&G researchers make that leap successfully, but the very fact that they did it across such diverse fields of knowledge makes the invention of fluoride toothpaste a breakthrough one.

The question is whether organizations only benefit from breakthrough or radical innovations. The answer is no. Each type of innovation has its definite place in the organization. Radical or breakthrough innovations produce step changes in organizations and the market it services. The printing press, iPod, Crest toothpaste, etc. are all examples of these kinds of innovation. But such radical or breakthrough innovations do not come about every day.

They have very long and often expensive incubation periods; the printing press took more than 20 years and fluoride toothpaste technology took 39 years to reach commercial production. An organization cannot devote 20 years of its time working on a single technology, however blockbuster it may seem. They are under pressure to improve on a daily basis to stay competitive. Most of these improvements come from small process changes that increase efficiency. A smart organization needs to manage a mix of various kinds of innovations to remain ahead of the game at every stage.

There have been organizations that have taken small improvements over a period of time to make great strides in quality, cost efficiency, and customer satisfaction. There may have been no one flashy big innovation but a series of small improvements that delivered significant competitive advantage. Nissan was the first Japanese car company and it was started in 1933. The second was Toyota in 1937. Toyota

The Indian Angle—ITC

ITC, originally the Indian Tobacco Company, was once upon a time a company that owned a blockbuster brand, Wills cigarettes and a chain of 5 star hotels. In more recent times, ITC has diversified into categories as wide and varied as wheat flour, sugar candy, biscuits, premium fashion apparel and information technology. However, no single initiative of ITC has made as much impact among more people than ITC's e-choupal movement.

The movement is the subject of case studies by Harvard Business School and the University of Michigan and is the 2004 winner of the World Business Award instituted jointly by the International Chamber of Commerce, the HRH Prince of Wales International Business Forum and the United Nations Development Program. The e-choupal sets up a marketplace for ITC to bypass middlemen when purchasing produce from farmers.

Then what's so special about the e-choupal? Because the method is breakthrough. Most farmers in India, if literate at all, know only their regional language. Physical infrastructure is poor with very few roads or even telephone lines. In that scenario, ITC has set up an internet based information network for a village where farmers can check the prices of his crop, order supplies or learn about global trends. E-choupal represents the global marketplace to a rural village.

Implemented in more than 11,000 villages, e-choupal results in lower procurement costs for ITC (though ITC guarantees a higher purchase price than the middlemen), higher realization for the farmers, better crop yield due to learning, better seeds and fertilizers, and has a rub-on effect for the entire village because of the availability of technology for school work and information from the

contd.

contd.

outside world. The variety of knowledge combined to produce e-choupal ranges from internet technology, hardware, VSAT, crop fertilizers, seed technology, commodity pricing and adult literacy. And the most significant result of e-choupal is rural empowerment.

created innovation in the car business. But their innovation was not in the car itself. It was in the manufacturing process.

In 1949, Toyota knew that they were in trouble. American car manufacturers like Ford had outstripped their production capacity by many times, leaving Toyota looking like a very poor cousin. The then president of Toyota, Kiichiro Toyoda, then offered a challenge to his team—to catch up with US production numbers—in the space of three years. The challenge was accepted by Taiichi Ohno, who along with Shigeo Shingo developed the Just-In-Time production system. They took the American car and started producing it with cheaper materials and more efficiently.

The Just-In-Time (JIT) production method relies on supplying every part of the production chain with only as much material as they need. At the end of the chain lies the customer who purchases a product which integrates all the way backward to raw materials—each part only arriving "Just-in-Time" for the next step. JIT lowered inventories and costs and therefore made Toyota more competitive. But they had to make a good car to begin with. The process improvements helped make Toyota one of the largest car manufacturers in the world today.

Incremental innovations can keep the engine going. But it is the big innovations that deliver the necessary impetus to keep an organization ahead of the pack. Perhaps the Toyota Corolla and the Prius represent the big changes that lead Toyota to where they are today.

The pursuit of breakthrough innovations also represents a higher risk, albeit with higher potential returns. The big bang innovations require huge investment of resources over a significant period of time. The small step innovations on the other hand have both small risk and small potential returns. An organization which is looking at building a balanced portfolio builds the optimal mix of both types.

In essence both kinds of innovations are required. The small steps help increase efficiency while the big innovation, when it comes, delivers the step change an organization needs to break away from competitors. The incremental innovations also help balance out the risk represented by the investment that goes into big bang innovations.

Is Innovation Episodic in Nature?
❀

Innovation is often perceived as episodic, coming and going in waves. It is something that does not happen often and is seen as a response to some stimuli. The typical innovation script is a grand solution developed to counter a problem. Necessity of circumstance leading to innovation has been the proverbial crutch of many innovations and inventions.

One such product born of necessity is the earmuff. In 1873, Chester Greenwood was a 15 year old boy in Maine whose ears became very cold in winter. Chester was allergic to wool and could not wrap his muffler around his head like most other people of the time. He put his mind at work one day and got his grandmother to make him a device that he designed. It had velvet on the inside, fur on the outside, and was strung around his head with wire. The earmuff was an instant hit. Soon every kid in town was demanding a Greenwood Champion Ear Protector. Necessity is sometimes a very young father of invention.

Crises can also create the environment that calls for innovation. This crisis can be internal, i.e. profitability linked, or external and part of the environment. Competition or economic scenarios lead organizations to innovate. Opportunities brought about by a changing environment can also be a trigger.

Table 1.1 lists the factors that distinguish Episodic innovation from Continuous innovation. A long-term investment is absolutely essential to ensure future competitiveness. The episodic form of innovation is inherently inefficient. It is reactive and often means that the organization is not the first to market. This can often create major upheaval in an organization while it scrambles to keep up with its competition.

Table 1.1: Episodic vs Continuous Innovation

	Episodic	Continuous
Trigger	Crisis/Change	Planning/Pro-active
Resource base	Contingent	Capabilities
Outcome	Radical/Upheaval	Evolutionary yet significant
Resource utilization	Wasteful	Optimal
Advantage bestowed	Temporary	Long term
Risk	High	Manageable

The resources spent to counter a crisis are not always spent in the most optimal manner and entail significant wastage that could otherwise be avoided with a planned program. This is brought about by the need to respond quickly. However, this upheaval and the immediate response is usually short-lived, as typically, once the crisis or change impulse passes the organization reverts to its old ways.

Then there is the pro-active approach.[2] Big bang innovations can be planned and delivered in a continuous manner. Efficiency led innovations can also be a part of the pipeline. The trigger here is not a change impulse or a crisis. It is, in fact, not a gun trigger at all. It is the planning and pro-active thinking that keeps the innovation pipeline ticking.

Organizations with a pro-active approach seek to be in the fore-front of the industry rather than play catch up. They regularly churn out a mix of innovations ranging from small improvements to potentially radical ones. They are more successful in the marketplace because they offer a greater variety of responses to the changing environment. Their chances of success thereby are greater. While Dupont as an organization is legendary for its invention of Nylon, Kevlar, Teflon, Lycra and other such materials that revolutionized fabric and material technology, Dupont hardly rested on its laurels in the intervening years. The organization put out a series of process improvements, technology improvements and material innovations to sharpen and hone its innovation abilities. Using Teflon, Dupont created several new products/technologies in areas as diverse as radar, nuclear weapons, and the household cooking pan.

Consistent with our knowledge view, these organizations build capabilities in the organization that enable combining or bringing together of disparate knowledge. The resource utilization is more likely to be efficient here, keeping the risk manageable. Given that the focus is on building lasting capabilities that deliver innovation or new knowledge, the organization should gain long-term competitive advantage. Organizations that aspire to deliver continuous yet significant innovations will have to develop an innovation capability which will be driven by constituent capabilities.

Conclusion
❀

Since the chapter began with Gutenberg, it is only fitting that it closes with another aspect of the Gutenberg innovation. This is the complexity involved in break-through innovation. The different kinds of knowledge and its integration makes the effort to put together the printing press a superhuman effort, one that Gutenberg dedicated most of his adult life to. This represents the frontier of what a single person can achieve. The world has become only more complex over the last 500 years or so. The era of individual innovator is well and truly over.

Most new knowledge is now being created in organizations, be it universities or large and small companies. The whole process of knowledge exchange and combination is a collaborative effort of a large number of people. What will make an organization innovative in this scenario? What capabilities would lead an organization to deliver continuous and significant innovations? The answers to these questions will give organizations lasting competitive advantage. It has often been said that innovation separates the winners of tomorrow from the losers. Consequently, the critical questions are what represents innovation capability for an organization and how is it built. The constituent capabilities that drive this overall innovation capability also need to be identified.

Key Takeouts
❀

- Creation of new knowledge equals innovation.
- New knowledge is created by bringing together

disparate types of knowledge in a unique, never done before manner.
- All types of innovation whether big or small are important for organizations.
- For lasting competitive advantage, the organizations need to build innovation capability or the ability to deliver continuous innovation.

Notes

1. Nahapiet, J. and S. Ghoshal. 1998. Social Capital, Intellectual Capital, and the Organizational Advantage. *Academy of Management Review*, 23(2), 242–66; Nonaka, I. and H. Takeuchi. 1995. *The Knowledge Creating Company: How Japanese Companies Create Dynamics of Innovation*. London: Oxford University Press; Drucker, P.F. 1998. The Discipline of Innovation. *Harvard Business Review*, November–December, 149–57.
2. Brown, S.L. and K.M. Eisenhardt. 1997. Art of Continuous Change: Linking Complexity Theory and Time Paced Evolution in Relentlessly Shifting Organizations. *Administrative Science Quarterly*, 42(1), 1–34.

Web Resources

1. www.ideafinder.com/history/inventors/gutenberg.htm
2. http://www.oneplusoneequalsthree.com/2004/05/western_movable. html
3. http://www.kdhprinting.com/inside/html/history.html
4. http://communication.ucsd.edu/bjones/Books/printech.html
5. http://www.computersmiths.com/chineseinvention/movtype.htm
6. http://www.valuebasedmanagement.net/methods_kaizen.html
7. http://www.1000ventures.com/business_guide/mgmt_kaizen_main. html
8. http://dandoweb.com/e/auto.html
9. http://www.pg.com/science/innovations_tartar.jhtml
10. http://www.ideafinder.com/history/inventions/story091.htm

11. http://inventors.about.com/od/wstartinventions/a/Walkman.htm
12. http://www.sony.net/Fun/SH/1-21/h1.html
13. http://www.osviews.com/modules.php?op=modload&name=News&
    file=article&sid=4259
14. http://www.fri.fujitsu.com/en/modules/popnupblog/index.php?param=
    3-20060320113506
15. http://media.wiley.com/product_data/excerpt/62/04717548/
    0471754862.pdf
16. http://www.digitaldividend.org/case/case_echoupal.htm
17. http://www.financialexpress.com/fe_full_story.php?content_id=59697

2 | Innovation as Capability

Innovation Tunnel ❋ *Innovation Capability* ❋ *Conclusion* ❋ *Key Takeouts*

Many organizations believe that to maintain an innovative culture, an organization needs to be small and flexible. They also believe in having expertize in a narrow arena. Large organizations are not seen as terribly creative, usually because of their unwieldy size that does not allow people to talk to each other across the organization. All that may be true, but it is also possible to be the opposite. Let us talk about 3M, which in popular belief, is one of the most innovative companies in the world. Here are some facts for the year ended 2005. 3M had a sales turnover of $34 bn and a profit margin of 15%, healthy by any standards. They also spent $1.2 bn on research and development and have 69,315 employees in 60 countries across the world. Yet this organization remained nimble and flexible enough to receive 487 US patents in 2005. In one single year. Now that is being innovative while being a large organization!

How do they manage it? 3M ensures sharing of knowledge and expertise. Not only is their primary research lab, Central Research staffed with people from various backgrounds like chemists, physicists, biologists; 3M also thrives in making them work together. 3M has Tech Forums where people can get together and share information and listen to experts like Nobel Laureates. The Tech Forums encourage teams to present their research problems to the forum and look for solutions jointly. They even gives out awards to inventors who are awarded patents.

The Tech Forum did not remain as a single unit either. It also created sub-groups of interest, such as polymers or coating processes. These sub-groups included people who were interested in the subject or were maybe struggling with some parts of it in their research. These scientists then pooled their expertize together to help solve each others' problems or spark ideas for themselves.

3M actively brought together different types of knowledge. When researchers developed a new product or refinement, they could not simply hand it over to sales and be done with it. Very often, due to 3M's freewheeling research methods, products or techniques were developed that had no obvious business application. In such cases, the scientist was made to pitch his/her invention to every possible product category, in the hope of finding one that could use the invention. Frequently, more than one use was found for the same product. Innovation found many homes through the sharing of knowledge at 3M.

3M did not stop at sharing knowledge within itself. They put into place several programs such as STEP (Science Training Encouragement Program) and 3M Visiting Wizards to interest and inspire students to take up science as an area of study. They also began programs to introduce teachers to science in industry. 3M is an organization that believes that innovation is a process that needs to be nurtured at every step of the way.

How was this culture of innovation put into place? One of 3M's early chairman William McKnight is credited for institutionalizing innovation long before other organizations began to understand its implications. McKnight believed very strongly that organizations need to support its employees and give them freedom to experiment. He offered employees the opportunity to make mistakes and an organization that encouraged them to think of solutions to solve every situation they came across. He created new teams like Products Fabrication Laboratory (Pro-Fab Labs) that had people who were creative and eccentric and who were given the freedom to work on projects that no one else had the time for. He created an organizational attitude that supported innovation.

McKnight also pioneered another department at 3M. One day, while evaluating the timeline of new products, McKnight realized that the rate of innovation was slowing down. He appreciated that it was necessary to have a constant flow of products through the innovation tunnel so that the process does not stop at any point. To this effect, he put together a New Products Department for the first time. The NPD had only one primary task—to evaluate research projects and markets and identify what would work where. NPD also had the power to fund or kill projects on the basis of their analysis and had to work in conjunction with production, sales and research. This NPD kept the 3M commitment to continuous innovation alive. McKnight did this in 1940. Sixty-six years later, many organizations are still struggling with their innovation tunnel.

The 3M story never ceases to amaze. What are some of the things that can be learnt from this truly inspirational organization? Very clearly there is knowledge involved. There are ways that they have developed to have diverse knowledge in their organization. They also exchange and use it better than most organizations. There is an element of culture or organizational attitude that drives this whole endeavor forward. The content of the whole process is the ability to have a lot of knowledge, and then the ability to combine it in a climate that is conducive to bringing knowledge together. These together represent an innovation capability of sorts.

Then there is an efficient process that they have put in place. That is the process of innovation tunnel. Let us tackle what this tunnel does for innovation first and then turn our attention to innovation capability of which the innovation tunnel is an important component.

Innovation Tunnel

❋

As in the 3M story, most organizations today have set up an innovation tunnel to efficiently monitor their progress in coming up with new business ideas. This tunnel is made for efficient sieving, sifting, and short-listing of potential ideas that can be taken forward. Often this is christened as the NPD or the new product development tunnel. The process works in multiple stages.[1]

Each stage of the tunnel has an evaluation system built into it. So ideas proceed to the next stage only if they fulfill these evaluation criteria. These set of criteria are built on suitability of the ideas to the organization, their business potential, and any competitive advantage that they may confer on the organization. This process is broadly called a stage-gate process. The ideas enter from one end, they are developed in various stages, where they have to pass through evaluation gates at each stage, and at the end of the process some of these ideas become products, services or processes that the organization can profit from.

One unlikely suspect that has a beautifully designed innovation tunnel is Royal Dutch/Shell. The offshoot of a shop that started out by importing seashells and exporting kerosene to Singapore and Bangkok in 1833, the Royal Dutch/Shell Group is today a $130 bn organization with over 102,000 employees. It was also a traditionally bureaucratic organization with a reputation for having mazes of brick walls between employees and departments. GameChanger began as an individual project by Tim Warren, the then director of research and technical services at the Exploration & Production group. It also began in 1996 with a problem that many managers are faced with today. Warren realized that the E&P division was not going to meet its earnings targets without some radical changes being made.

Even though the problem is a familiar one, what Warren did is what finally changed the game at Shell. Warren put a team of key people together across his department and gave them the sole power to solicit ideas and fund projects to the tune of $20 mn. That's right. Not a $100,000. Not $1 mn. But $20 mn! The GameChanger process began in November 1996, but as typical of bureaucratic organizations, most employees were so used to thinking a certain way that they had difficulty in coming up with rule breaking ideas for the GameChanger panel.

The GameChanger team then hired a bunch of consultants and put together a series of innovation labs. Once again, anyone across the organization could attend the innovation lab and the carrot was an on-the-spot dole of $500,000 to ideas that made the grade. Seventy-two people turned up and they brainstormed and used several ideation techniques to come up with a laundry list of 240 ideas that could be worked on. These included ideas for new businesses and new approaches to existing departments.

The teams, however, did not stop with ideation. They then devised a set of stage-gate criteria to decide which ideas would qualify for funding. The teams also selected 12 ideas from the laundry list to be taken forward and given the seed money funding for development. These 12 ideas once again gathered volunteers around it who would work on them at every step of the rest of the way.

The ideas and teams were then put through a 5-day lab that scoped out the ideas, financial implications, competitive information, and the operating boundaries. They were also given 100 days to develop a low-risk, low-cost method of testing their business plan. At the end of that time, they presented their plans to the GameChanger panel for further sponsorship and support. The ideas typically ended up with the appropriate departments within Shell as a fully fledged business initiative.

Did the GameChanger process translate into business success? Absolutely. In 1999, just two short years after the first GameChanger panel was set up, four out of Shell's five major new business initiatives were products of GameChanger. GameChanger projects were receiving as much as 30% of the Exploration & Production group's R&D budget.

Today the process has become institutionalized. On a fairly well hidden section of Shell's website, the GameChanger panel solicits ideas from outsiders as well as employees. They invite proposals to go through a very similar stage-gate process as the first GameChanger process. If the organization or person giving the idea is an outsider, then they can be invited to become suppliers, licensors, development partners, or even have Shell invest in their company. This process can be translated across almost any organization or department.

Shell knows that they need to keep the flow coming at the entrance of the innovation tunnel. Broadly speaking, the stages in an innovation tunnel can be grouped into four. The first stage is idea generation. Here the organization casts a wide net to get as many ideas as possible. The techniques may range from formal brainstorming sessions to inviting ideas from employees in general. In some organizations, formal presentations may also be conducted.

The second stage comes after the ideas with most potential have been shortlisted. This list can either be developed by doing a quick idea sort with customers/consumers or on an internal checklist. In the second stage, the idea is actually developed further. A business plan may start to develop, all potential applications may be explored, and potential markets, etc. may start to fructify. Incubated ideas are again sieved and

Figure 2.1: Innovation Tunnel

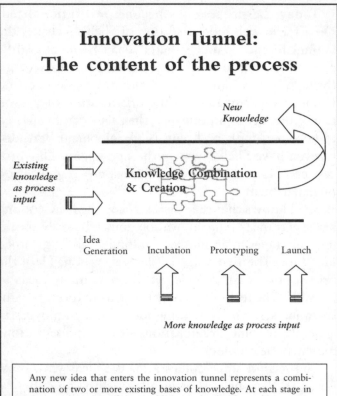

Any new idea that enters the innovation tunnel represents a combination of two or more existing bases of knowledge. At each stage in the tunnel new knowledge is added to make the idea viable commercially.

At the heart of this process that many companies use is knowledge. Organizations possessing a large knowledge base, and the ability as well as a conducive environment to combine this knowledge in unique ways would exploit this process most efficiently.

then led into prototyping. Prototyping is the third stage, and here the ideas will actually be put in physical form and tested in real market or application situations. This is an important stage as it determines which ideas can set the marketplace on fire in the last stage.

For a successful program it is important that at each stage of evaluation, learning is taken on board and the idea is constantly worked upon. This rigorous development of an idea ensures its final success or failure.

The stage-gate process is a good one to monitor, control, and reduce uncertainty in the innovation process. However, that is just one aspect of the whole innovation setup. What flows through this tunnel and how it gets transformed into ideas is also equally important. The raw material of this tunnel is knowledge (see Figure 2.1). Ideas represent nothing but interesting combinations of existing knowledge. The output is knowledge itself, new knowledge that competitors do not have and confers competitive advantage on the organization.

There are a few things to note here. The organization needs to possess knowledge assets that competitors do not have in order come up with truly interesting and unique ideas. These ideas are raw materials and have to be of high quality. The organizational climate needs to then help bring together the different ideas. At each evaluation stage new increments of knowledge are added. Again the knowledge assets, organizational attitude, and ability to combine knowledge become important.

Focus on process alone can have detrimental effects. If the organization does not put in good raw material, the new knowledge created may not be very useful. In fact, the organization also needs enabling infrastructure to be able to combine knowledge effectively.

Innovation Capability
❋

How does one define innovation capability? It can be viewed as the ability to come up, consistently, with new knowledge that delivers short and long-term profits to an organization.[2] This new knowledge is in the form of novel business ideas that could result in new products/ services, efficient business processes, or exploiting of new markets.

There are two parts of this capability. One part is the process and the other part is the asset.[3] Process is usually represented by the innovation tunnel. It represents the physical process of processing raw materials for innovation. The asset part is all about the raw materials and infrastructure that go into the process.

Very clearly, in order to produce new knowledge a large reservoir of existing knowledge is required. P&G is one organization that has devised a good way for unlocking the knowledge that resides within its 98,000 employees. P&G has an organization-wide platform called MyINet that performs two tasks. The first is that it hosts a searchable database of over 2 million research documents from P&G labs across the world. The documents are made searchable in such a way that researchers can cull out information that is relevant to their field of study from every part of the organization's research documents. This helps in translating knowledge from one application area to another as well.

P&G also has an interactive service called Ask Me on MyINet. Ask Me is actually the initial thought behind MyINet and its success led to the creation of MyINet. Ask Me is a service where researchers can post queries or problems that they are facing in their work. Researchers across the P&G world, regardless of department, have access to the queries posted and can answer, guide or refer them to experts. Apart from the researchers, P&G also has a team of technical entrepreneurs within the organization whose task is to attend conferences, technical programs, and work with universities and the Internet to identify and internalize knowledge that can further P&G's innovation goals. One of which is that 50% of the innovation within P&G must have an external root to it.

Similarly, any good organization should have the ability to scan the environment for new knowledge and be able to absorb it. Knowledge represents both the raw material and infrastructure. It can be seen as infrastructure because it helps absorb new knowledge.[4] (How that happens is tackled in subsequent chapters.) The organizational environment aids combination of this knowledge. The organizational attitude in some ways is the enabling infrastructure for innovation capability. The key question that this capability asks is whether the organization has the right attitude that enables playful combination of knowledge.

P&G's MyINet would never be of any use unless its researchers actually put it to the test. Most organizations put into place intranet knowledge bases without any premium being placed on its use. Researchers at P&G actively search for knowledge that will help them in areas other than their own areas of research. How else would detergent and hard water research lead to fluoride toothpaste and calcium supplements or soap and candle making lead to vegetable shortening?

The organization must possess the inherent ability to be able to bring together these bases of knowledge and combine them. Systems and processes that help sharing of knowledge and help force different bases of knowledge together is the tunnel's key infrastructure. Tools and techniques that effectively bring together different types of knowledge are also a part of this infrastructure.

The fact that an organization needs to possess a variety of abilities/capabilities (e.g. knowledge bases, environment as enabling infrastructure and ability to combine knowledge) to effectively and continuously innovate means that innovation capability has constituent capabilities. These capabilities together determine the innovation capability of the organization. (See Figure 2.2). They can be grouped under three broad capabilities that together determine the innovation capability of an organization.

Figure 2.2: Building Innovation Capability

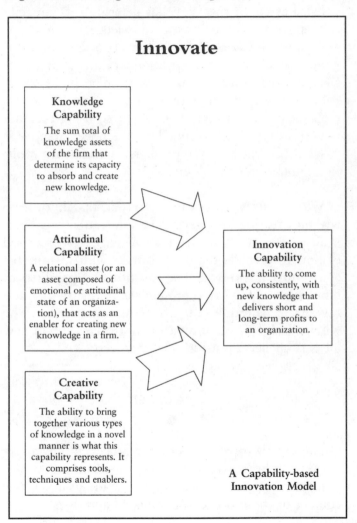

Innovate

Knowledge Capability

The sum total of knowledge assets of the firm that determine its capacity to absorb and create new knowledge.

Attitudinal Capability

A relational asset (or an asset composed of emotional or attitudinal state of an organiza- tion), that acts as an enabler for creating new knowledge in a firm.

Creative Capability

The ability to bring together various types of knowledge in a novel manner is what this capability represents. It comprises tools, techniques and enablers.

Innovation Capability

The ability to come up, consistently, with new knowledge that delivers short and long-term profits to an organization.

A Capability-based Innovation Model

- **Knowledge Capability:**[5] The sum total of knowledge assets of the firm that determine its capacity to absorb and create new knowledge.
- **Attitudinal Capability:**[6] This is a relational asset (or an asset composed of emotional or attitudinal state of an organization), that acts as an enabler for creating new knowledge in a firm.
- **Creative Capability:**[7] The ability to bring together various types of knowledge in a novel manner is what this capability represents. It comprises tools, techniques and enablers.

What is amply clear by now is the fact that innovation is about creating knowledge and innovation capability is about effectively creating knowledge over a period of time to provide the organization with sustainable competitive advantage. The constituent capabilities of innovation capability represent the infrastructure and raw materials required to create new knowledge. The whole black box on innovation or the creation of new ideas is opened up using this approach.

Conclusion
❀

Often organizations focus on the process of any activity. What is borrowed from other organizations as best practice is often the process of getting things done. The content of these processes is missed and does not get transferred. As a result, the record of best practice transfer is pretty patchy. A lot of companies have the innovation tunnel implemented in their organizations but few will have it working as well as 3M to have 487 patents in a year. The process is extremely important but not the only determinant of success. There are raw materials and infrastructure that need to be in place for the process to work. The challenge an organization faces is to put these in place along with the process.

The process ensures efficiency and the content ensures effectiveness. The best way to make this capability work is to make sure that both process and content are in fine shape. The focus of the knowledge-based view in this book is on the content of this capability.

Even from a content view, innovation capability is a multifaceted capability that has at least three constituent capabilities. The organization needs to work on all three of these to deliver continuous and significant innovation. The following chapters go into the details of these three and provides directions to build these capabilities in the organization.

Key Takeouts

- Innovation capability of an organization comprises both process and content.
- Focus on process alone may not deliver optimal results.

- The content part of innovation capability consists of three constituent capabilities.
- All three of these constituent capabilities of an organization need to be developed to deliver a continuous stream of new knowledge or innovation.

Notes

1. Tranfield, D., M. Young, D. Partington, J. Bessant and J. Sapsed. 2003. Knowledge Management Routines for Innovation Projects: Developing a Hierarchical Process Model. *International Journal of Innovation Management*, 7(1), 27–49; O'Connor, G.C. and A.D. Ayers. 2005. Building Radical Innovation Capability. *Research Technology Management*, 48(1), 23–32; Davila, T., M.J. Epstein and R. Shelton. 2006. *Making Innovation Work*. New Jersey: Wharton School Publishing.
2. Parashar M. and Sunil Kr. Singh. 2005. Innovation Capability. *Management Review*, 17(4), 115–23.
3. Teece, D.J. and G. Pisano. 1994. The Dynamic Capability of Firms: An Introduction. *Industrial and Corporate Change*, 3(3), 537–56; Teece, D.J., G. Pisano and A. Shuen. 1997. Dynamic Capabilities and Strategic Management. *Strategic Management Journal*, 18(7), 509–33.
4. Cohen, W.M. and D.A. Levinthal. 1990. Absorptive Capacity: A New Perspective on Learning and Innovation. *Administrative Science Quarterly*, 35(1), 128–52.
5. Parashar M. and Sunil Kr. Singh. 2005.
6. Parashar M. and Sunil Kr. Singh. 2005.
7. Parashar M. and Sunil Kr. Singh. 2005.

Web Resources

1. http://www.3m.com
2. http://www.referenceforbusiness.com/management/Gr-Int/Innovation.html
3. http://solutions.3m.com/wps/portal/!ut/p/kcxml/04_Sj9SPykssy0x PLMnMz0vM0Q9KzYsPDdaP0I8yizeIDwrQL8hwVAQABzAF5w!!

4. http://www.businessweek.com/2000/00_38/b3699129.htm
5. http://www.businessweek.com/1999/99_50/b3659021.htm
6. http://hbswk.hbs.edu/item.jhtml?id=1444&t=innovation
7. http://www.strategos.com/articles/internalmkts/markets4.htm
8. http://www.shell.com/home/Framework?siteId=gamechanger-en&FC2=/gamechanger-en/html/iwgen/leftnavs/zzz_lhn2_0_0.html&FC3=/gamechanger-en/html/iwgen/about_shell/introduction.html

3 | Knowing

There is another organization that is legendary for its commitment to innovation and the systematic pursuit of it. DuPont is responsible for creating several innovative products in its portfolio like Neoprene, Nylon, Lycra, Dacron and Teflon. The DuPont commitment to research dates back to the early 1900s where the first R&D department was set up. Typical of the times, when many of the research projects failed to come to fruition, one of the two cousins who ran the company,

Alfred I. Dupont, started questioning the need for R&D. However, Cousin Pierre Dupont ensured that Dupont R&D survived, and to this day, it has flourished.

In 1926, Charles Stine, the director of DuPont's Central Research department put up a proposal to undertake pure research or fundamental research. He asked for funds to hire researchers who would then work on chemical problems that interested them without any pressure on practical applications. Stine believed that practical applications would follow automatically. Dupont's commitment to R&D investment led to them approving far more money to follow his project than Stine had even dreamt of.

Stine's first two recruits were Alan Coburn and Wallace Carothers. Both proved to be blockbuster finds as Coburn developed the field of chemical engineering and eventually set up a department at the University of Delaware. Carothers came on board and flourished too in the open environment, and quickly created the breakthrough that would result in neoprene. Carothers was also working on a new artificial fiber but had several technical problems with it. He eventually set it aside and tried to work on something else. At the time, a new director was brought to Central Research, Elmer Bolton, who believed that practical applications were essential for fundamental research. Bolton believed that Carothers was on to something with his new fiber research and kept pushing him to deliver results. The pressure worked and Carothers eventually developed the fiber that would be called nylon in 1937.

Dupont's focus on research that worked continued through the post-World War II era. By then nylon was a hugely popular fabric. Yet constant consumer research showed that in a time where washing machines were making life easier for women by taking over laundry, there was one task that was still painful for women—Ironing. Dupont, never one to leave a market opportunity alone, developed a wash-and-wear, wrinkle-resistant fabric—dacron.

Dupont also took the step of involving key customers in their R&D process. Large numbers of customers were invited along with R&D and marketing teams to incorporate both marketing and consumer insights into the research process. This ensured that a greater proportion of work was done in areas that had its roots in information from the market and consumers, and therefore, a greater chance to succeed. Dupont is extremely aware of the fact that in the chemical industry, innovation must be based on consumer and customer insight as well as their research-based knowledge. If they depend solely on research output, then they face the risk of commoditization and incremental innovation that may leave Dupont by the wayside in the marketplace.

Dupont also believed in the sharing of knowledge. It took the extremely unusual step (for a money-making corporation, at least) of publishing its research in academic journals. These led to other academic minds being able to study and further research the various scientific projects that interested them. Charlie Pedersen, a chemist at Dupont was even awarded a Nobel Prize in Chemistry.

Dupont does not stop at publishing its knowledge in the academic domain. It also runs a program in its Crop Protection unit called University Compounds. University Compounds asks researchers to send Dupont samples of molecular compounds that they are working on. In case Dupont finds them interesting, Dupont will offer to buy the compounds off the researcher and undertake their own testing. If the tests look positive then the researcher may be invited to participate in a research cooperation program. Dupont claims that new products now contribute to 33% of Dupont revenues and the goal is to make that figure 35%. The way Dupont has been managing their innovation process, it seems very likely that they will get there sooner than later.

Some very important learning emerges out of this Dupont example. This particular organization seems to be building some very important reservoirs of knowledge. As has been argued before, the richer and more diverse these reservoirs of knowledge are, the greater the chance of being able to combine them and come up with new knowledge. Investments in R&D help build large reservoirs of technical knowledge that can absorb new knowledge. Consumer knowledge is built through a robust program of consumer research. Often it is said that when consumer knowledge is combined with technical knowledge, the results will be more successful and more profitable than innovations based only on one or the other.

Knowledge Capability

❁

If an organization wishes to form new combinations of knowledge, then it needs to have a diverse set of knowledge bases. These knowledge bases also help absorb new knowledge.[1] The notion is simple. One needs to know multiplication first to be able to do mathematical operations like square roots or calculus. These two roles of knowledge, of sustaining itself and attracting new knowledge, make it very important for continuous innovation in the organization. Knowledge reservoirs then represent a constituent capability of innovation capability. This capability can thus be defined as the sum total of knowledge assets of the firm that determine its capacity to absorb and create new knowledge.

Knowledge resides in various forms. The most common classification is explicit knowledge (codified) and tacit knowledge (resides in people).[2] The explicit form of knowledge is the kind of knowledge that can be codified into documents, manuals and databases. This kind of knowledge is thus easy to transfer. Also, this knowledge forms the foundation of the knowledge capability of an organization. The greater the documented store of knowledge that is easy to access and use, the greater the chance that continuous innovation will happen.

There is also knowledge that is difficult to codify, and hence only resides in people who possess it. This kind of knowledge can be in the form of special skills or in the form of heuristics used for decision-making. These are essentially thumb rules that people develop with personal experience or through anecdotal evidence of other people. Everybody possesses heuristics about their jobs or skills. Anyone who has to work with the government will see the best evidence of heuristics— the formal rules for getting something done is often very different from the practical way to approach it.

However, when a new person enters a job, then while the explicit knowledge is often passed on, it is the heuristics involved that rarely get translated explicitly. The challenge with heuristics and special skills is two-fold, one, to bring it out as explicit knowledge and second, to make it possible to combine it with other kinds of knowledge.[3]

There is another kind of knowledge that exists among groups of people. This is the notion of social capital, which is defined as resources embedded in relationships.[4] These resources are usually knowledge resources. Having a variety of relationships increases the access that an organization has to external knowledge reservoirs.

The question is that how does an organization ensure that it has enough knowledge reservoirs to keep the innovation tunnel buzzing? The most direct way is to consciously look at the three kinds of knowledge and deliberately build reservoirs based on these kinds of knowledge. In the following section some important ways to build bases of knowledge are discussed.

The Indian Angle—Infosys

Infosys is the brand that stands for Indian IT in many eyes. One of the earliest software companies to pioneer its 'Global Delivery Model' Infosys has a turnover of US $2,152 mn and it is only celebrating its 25th anniversary in 2006. With 52,175 employees in offices all the way from Atlanta to Zurich, with Bangalore & Utrecht thrown in, Infosys is truly a global company. So how does this global company ensure that all its employees are on the same page with each other and their customers? By building its knowledge capability.

Infosys is an organization that has made great strides in managing and using its knowledge capabilities. As a consulting company, Infosys places a premium on building knowledge pools across divisions and levels. To this end, they have put into place several practices such as regular workshops, white papers, seminars, webinars, etc. that ensure that knowledge is recorded and shared.

Infosys has also been recognized for its knowledge capability. In 2005, it was inducted into the Most Admired Knowledge Enterprises (MAKE) Hall of Fame. MAKE is a research program that researches and acknowledges the best practice knowledge organizations globally. Infosys happens to be the only Indian company inducted into the Hall of Fame.

Infosys' knowledge networks are not restricted only to its own organization. A 2002 agreement with IBM ensures that employees create knowledge across the two organizations through IBM's software developer platforms and Infosys' knowledge management intranet.

Infosys knows very well, that in the knowledge economy, it is the company that can mine and use its knowledge capability that will end up as the winner of

contd.

contd.

the game. Infosys does all the necessary things—recruiting a diverse workforce across nationalities and skill sets, building internal and external networks to access knowledge, doing R&D to sustain new knowledge, learn about consumers and customers alike, and create new programs to ensure the dissemination of knowledge. In these respects, Infosys is truly a knowledge company.

Diverse Workforce

As already discussed people possess knowledge that is not easily codifiable. Hiring people with the kinds of skills and experience that an organization requires is the sure-fire way to build non-codifiable knowledge within the organization.[5] Recruitment procedures geared towards building work groups with diverse skill-sets will ensure that a better cross-section of non-codifiable knowledge will be represented.

Apart from non-codifiable knowledge there is a great deal of knowledge that exists in people that may be codified with effort, but there is a huge cost involved in doing so. This knowledge comes from their background, their experiences; the various degrees or types of education they possess; social, religious and ethnic backgrounds also provide special knowledge to people. Even the out-of-office interests that people possess endow them with distinct knowledge. If organizations can hire people keeping an eye on a heterogeneous mix of people, then the cause of innovation will be served.[6] Homogenous set of employees may result in a comfortable but non-creative environment. This non-creative environment may be great for efficiency or training ease. But if the overlap of knowledge is high, it is unlikely that there will be enough knowledge diversity for new knowledge to be created.

Consumer/Customer Knowledge

A deep understanding of the consumer provides a strong base for innovation.[7] This understanding does not come from normal market research that is done to validate pending decisions. Product tests, advertising tests or simulated test markets while important to help make informed decisions, provide very little information that can result in promoting a deep understanding of the consumer. While validation is necessary at various points of the marketing cycle, the organization needs to take an exploratory approach to market research to sustain the spirit of innovation.

There are some techniques that explore the consumer psyche in depth, and there are also techniques that bring out the social aspect of consumer behavior. Techniques borrowed from other social sciences like ethnography and phenomenology are useful in understanding behavior in social contexts. Techniques from psychology like projective techniques explore the consumer psyche. Pure observation tactics represented by un-obtrusive methods provide a different view into the life

Figure 3.1: Building Knowledge Capability

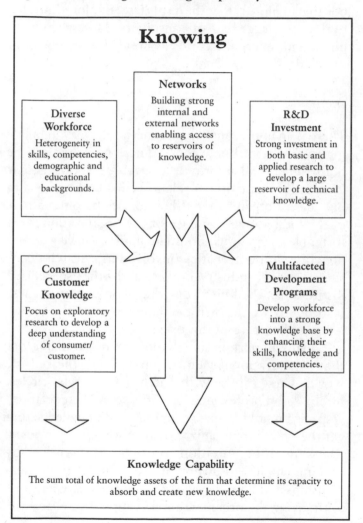

Knowing

Networks

Building strong internal and external networks enabling access to reservoirs of knowledge.

Diverse Workforce

Heterogeneity in skills, competencies, demographic and educational backgrounds.

R&D Investment

Strong investment in both basic and applied research to develop a large reservoir of technical knowledge.

Consumer/ Customer Knowledge

Focus on exploratory research to develop a deep understanding of consumer/ customer.

Multifaceted Development Programs

Develop workforce into a strong knowledge base by enhancing their skills, knowledge and competencies.

Knowledge Capability

The sum total of knowledge assets of the firm that determine its capacity to absorb and create new knowledge.

of consumers and customers. The idea is to use methods that explore rather than validate. Exploration adds to the knowledge base of consumers. This, when combined with internal technical knowledge, can provide novel ideas.

Networks

There is an important role that networks play in building reservoirs of knowledge.[8] These networks can be both formal and informal. The whole notion is that knowledge that exists in relationships both inside and outside the organizational boundaries becomes a part of the total knowledge base of the organization. At a formal level attempts should be made to have a strong network with universities (involved in research), consumer bodies, industry bodies, and other specialized institutions. The knowledge that would exist in these institutions would then become a part of the knowledge architecture of the organization.

Equally important are the informal socializing ties that organizational members have with the outside world. These can be with batch mates, social circles, hobby clubs, professional societies, etc. These relationships again hold immense amounts of knowledge that can be used for organizational innovation purposes. The way an organization can make this work is by making employees aware of the value of these relationships and how they can further their careers along with giving the organization a competitive edge.

Then the networks within the organization also play a role. But that role is in terms of sharing and combining knowledge. They are important for the final coming with innovative ideas phase.

R&D Investment

Most innovative organizations spend a significant percentage of their turnover on research. P&G spends about 3.5% of worldwide sales on R&D. For Dupont that figure is about 4.9%. 3M has an even higher percentage of sales spend of about 5.8%. This is largely because investment in R&D helps build technical knowledge base. Now this investment can be in basic research or in applied research. This would depend on the kind of strategy that the organization follows. If the organization is looking at making fundamental changes in the business environment through breakthrough products and services, investment in basic research has to be fairly high. 3M is an organization that has historically encouraged basic research. The purpose of 3M's Pro-Fab Lab was to work on basic research that could turn up interesting ideas. These interesting ideas need not have been related to any existing 3M project, product or initiative. However, if the researcher at the time felt that there was an application possible from his research, then he could pitch it to any of the 3M divisions for further funding and development. 3M calls this kind of research as fuzzy front end research. At the time that the research is undertaken, no one knows whether there will be any useful application developed from it. Yet 3M researchers can keep going at it for months, even years until they figure out something of interest. In 1944, 3M acquired the rights to a process for creating fluorochemical compounds. At the time and for 12 years after that, no one had figured out what to do with the compounds. But 3M persevered with the technology and in 1952 Patsy Sherman began the research that would lead to the launch of Scotchgard in 1956.

Even if the intention is to use basic research from somewhere else and apply it to solutions, the organization necessarily has to invest in applied research. Today the rate of technical change is pretty fast and technology itself is complex. Any organization that needs to utilize a new technical advancement needs to have a basic understanding of technology. That understanding cannot be formed without investment in applied R&D.

Even an imitating strategy needs a basic understanding of what is being imitated. If an organization A invests $50 million dollars on a new technology and launches a consumer product for it, many companies can try and imitate it. So if organization B wants to make a cheap knock-off, it still needs to be able to take apart the product and recreate it. Imitators therefore have to invest in basic technical knowledge. Presence of in-house technical knowledge not only helps create new knowledge or innovations but also helps absorb new technical knowledge from outside.[9]

The Indian Angle—Tata Motors

Tata Motors, formerly known as Tata Engineering & Locomotive Co. Ltd. or Telco is one of the grand-daddies of the Indian automotive industry. Yet, the organization had never forayed into passenger cars until its launch of the 'India Car' Indica in 1998.

The thought behind the Indica shows the root of the quest that Tata Motors embarked on with innovation. The company's management were challenged by Ratan Tata to build a car that had all the characteristics of the best cars in the market at the time and deliver it to the consumer at the lowest price possible. Tata Motors had to look around for inexpensive R&D in an industry dominated by MNCs that had decades of passenger car experience and the budgets to match.

In this effort, Tata Motors launched the Indica. However, the Indica too was not the overnight success that it was supposed to be. Tata Motors then went back to the drawing board and worked on the car all over again.

The second time around, they got the formula right and the Indica was relaunched with great success. Today, Tata Motors has its lessons down right. Its investment in R&D has increased from 1% of sales in 2004 to as much as 2.2% of sales in 2005.

Famously a straight-laced organization, Tata Motors has also adopted the procedure of assembling cross-functional groups from different departments that work together. These teams come together to work on deputation from their departments on new ideas. The types of projects are wide and varied, and significantly, for an Indian company, not all of them have immediate applicability. Tata Motors realizes the importance of building knowledge capability in the organization to ensure that it remains equipped for the future.

Multifaceted Development Programs

Organizations can actively increase their total knowledge base by developing the knowledge capability of the workforce.[10] The ways in which this can be achieved are many. The fundamental way is to expose them to new knowledge through training programs. These could be in-house, or to maximize benefits, could be in leading educational institutions. Exposing organizational members to new and varied experiences can also help development of this capability.

As an organization there could be an emphasis on creating special interest groups that work not only on organizational problems, but enhance the overall understanding of subject matter. P&G's technical entrepreneurs focus solely on gathering outside knowledge on research topics and disseminating that knowledge to P&G researchers. They attend seminars, forums and training to actively collect this outside information and material. MyINet in P&G remains as an active source of information and research, both from within P&G and from the outside world. There could even be communities of practice headed by masters from within or outside the organization that instill new tacit knowledge in people.

Conclusion
❁

Knowledge capability is the fundamental capability that an organization needs to build to be able to innovate on a continuous basis. Knowledge itself is the raw material of innovation. If there are many diverse kinds of raw materials available, they can be put together in countless new ways to deliver a continuous stream of finished product, i.e. new knowledge or innovation. Organizations have to deliberately build reservoirs of knowledge to be able to become truly innovative organizations.

A robust knowledge capability will also ensure that the organization is able to absorb new knowledge from the external world effectively. This would lead to a virtuous cycle of ever expanding knowledge capability. Long-term competitive advantage for the firm then is truly assured. What is required is an appreciation that knowledge is at the base of all innovation.

Key Takeouts

❋

- Knowledge capability is fundamental to the overall innovation capability of a firm.
- Three kinds of knowledge—explicit, tacit and the one existing in relationships are all required to build knowledge capability.
- Investment in consumer knowledge and R&D build reservoirs of explicit knowledge.
- Networks exploit the knowledge present in relationships.

- A diverse workforce and multifaceted development programs are keys to building a big base of knowledge in the organization at a tacit level.

Notes

1. Cohen, W.M. and D.A. Levinthal. 1990. Absorptive Capacity: A New Perspective on Learning and Innovation. *Administrative Science Quarterly*, 35(1), 128–52.
2. Nonaka, I. and H. Takeuchi. 1995. *The Knowledge Creating Company: How Japanese Companies Create Dynamics of Innovation*. London: Oxford University Press; Polanyi, M. 1967. *The Tacit Dimension*. New York: Doubleday.
3. Nonaka, I. and H. Takeuchi, 1995.
4. Coleman, J.S. 1988. Social Capital in the Creation of Human Capital. *American Journal of Sociology*, 94(5), 95–120; Nahapiet, J. and S. Ghoshal. 1998. Social Capital, Intellectual Capital and the Organizational Advantage. *Academy of Management Review*, 23(2), 242–66; A. Portes. 1998. Social Capital: Its Origins and Applications in Modern Sociology. *Annual Review of Sociology*, 24, 1–24.
5. Ghoshal, S. and C.A. Bartlett. 1997. *The Individualized Corporation: A Fundamentally New Approach to Management*. New York: HarperBusiness.
6. Thompson, L. 2003. Improving the Creativity of Organizational Work Groups. *Academy of Management Executive*, 17(1), 96–111.
7. Marinova, D. 2004. Actualizing Innovation: The Impact of Market Knowledge Diffusion in a Dynamic System of Competition. *Journal of Marketing*, 68(3), 1–20; Desouza, K.C. and Y. Awazu. 2004. Gaining a Competitive Edge from Your Customers: Exploring the Three Dimensions of Customer Knowledge. *KM Review*, 7(3), 12–15; Brown, S. and K.M. Eisenhardt. 1995. Product Development: Past Research, Present Findings and Future Directions. *Academy of Management Review*, 20(2), 343–78.
8. Powell, W.W., K.W. Koput, and L. Smith-Doerr. 1996. Inter-organizational Collaboration and the Locus of Innovation: Networks of Learning in Biotechnology. *Administrative Science Quarterly*, 41(1), 116–45; Tsai W. and S. Ghoshal 1998. Social Capital and Value

Creation: Role of Intra-firm Networks. *Academy of Management Journal*, 41(4), 464–71.

9. Cohen, W.M. and D.A. Levinthal. 1990. Absorptive Capacity: A New Perspective on Learning and Innovation. *Administrative Science Quarterly*, 35(1), 128–52.

10. Roffe, I. 1999. Innovation and Creativity in Organizations: A Review of the Implications for Training and Development. *Journal of European Industrial Training*, 23(4), 224–37.

Web Resources

1. http://www.heritage.dupont.com, DuPont: The Enlightened Organization by Dr. John Kenly Smith, Associate Professor of History at Lehigh University and Co-Author of *Science and Corporate Strategy, DuPont R&D, 1902 to 1980.*

2. http://pubs.acs.org/cen/coverstory/83/8316specialtychem.html

3. http://www.williammcdermott.com/proctor_and_gamble.pdf

4. http://www.businessweek.com/magazine/content/04_41/b3903463.htm

5. http://www.ugs.com/about_us/success/pg.shtml

6. http://www.intel.com/cd/ids/developer/asmona/eng/strategy/retail/52546.htm

7. http://www.intel.com/business/casestudies/pg_research.pdf http://www.askmecorp.com/press/jul16.asp

8. http://www.baselinemag.com/article2/0,1540,1620221,00.asp

9. http://www.fastcompany.com/magazine/95/design-qa.html

10. http://www.msnbc.msn.com/id/7856259/site/newsweek/

11. http://hbswk.hbs.edu/item.jhtml?id=5258&t=innovation&iss=y

12. http://www.expressitpeople.com/20020812/careers4.shtml

13. http://www.destinationkm.com/articles/default.asp?ArticleID=982

14. http://www.infosys.com/media/press_releases/global-make-award-hall-of-fame.asp

15. http://www.infosys.com/about/quick_facts.asp

16. http://rediff.co.in/money/2005/nov/19spec.htm

17. http://www.tata.com/tata_motors/articles/20040925_tata_motors.htm

18. http://knowledge.wharton.upenn.edu/index.cfm?fa=viewArticle&id=1275

19. http://www.tata.com/tata_motors/articles/20030802_crash_testing.htm

20. http://www.tata.com/tata_motors/articles/20030825_challenge.htm
21. http://www.tatamotors.com/our_world/press_releases.php? ID=227& action=Pull
22. http://www.tatamotors.com/our_world/press_releases.php?ID= 192&action=Pull
23. http://www.tatamotors.com/our_world/research.php
24. http://domain-b.com/companies/companies_t/tcs/20041208_deal.html
25. http://www.tata.com/tata_motors/articles/20030424_rebuilding_ success_stories.htm
26. http://www.cfoasia.com/archives/200512-01.htm

4 | Attitude

Incorporated in 1998, Google's beginnings were typical to the start-ups of the time. Graduate students Larry Page and Sergey Brin met when Page visited Brin's campus at Stanford. On the tour, they started arguing about current search technology and the sparks flew. By January 1996, they had begun collaboration on a search engine called Back Rub. By 1998, they had perfected their technology and were looking for partners to license from them. They could not find any takers, and finally were encouraged to start the company themselves. They began by pitching to Andy Bechtolsheim, the founder of Sun Microsystems. And they got a check for $100,000 in funding before they even had a company or a name for it. The check was made out in the name of Google Inc and so that's what they named the company. Yet this start-up was getting over 100,000 hits before it was six months old, and has been profitable since 2001.

Google now has almost 5,000 employees in offices across the world. The company is known for its innovation culture and its ability to deliver breakthrough innovation. Google desktop and Gmail have had industry biggies running for cover. It has become iconic as an employer and they claim to receive almost 1,000 applications a day. What makes Google so special?

Google, though a very young organization, has defined its market at a very broad level. The founders define their market as being "about search." It's possible when you have a search engine and you are "about search," that the focus of your organization will be on making your search engine better, faster, and more loaded. But Google has turned that logic on its head. Their approach is to find newer products that they can load their search technology onto. Approached from that point of view, Google immediately found a wide range of products and technology that could help them expand their business. Google has been quick to adapt, adopt, or even buy into other technology.

Google keeps the innovation flow going by letting its employees work on things that interest them. There is a list of Top 100 priorities and engineers choose projects that they want to work on. They get together in interest groups and work together for days, weeks or months until the project is completed. Particularly outlandish projects are specially marked out to ensure that they are not judged or evaluated at that particular stage. They are developed bias-free until they become feasible.

One such experiment is Krishna Bharat's dynamic news service. Bharat believed that Google could provide a news service that would be dynamically updated every hour from different sources. Bharat simply sent out an internal email about his project to his co-workers. One of them, Marissa Mayer thought that his idea was interesting enough to merit a trial and in six weeks Google News was up. Within three weeks of launch Google News had 70,000 users.

Today, it is a fact that there are very few domains on the Internet that have not been penetrated by Google's efficiency at search. Websites, books, images, desktops, maps, satellite images, shopping catalogues, emails and chat conversations all can be searched by Google's power. Google even sells advertising based on the location of the user so that it is better targeted.

What are the factors that make companies like Google special? It is to an extent that they react as an organization to new ideas, new knowledge and problem solving. This is a kind of reflex that the organization displays. It is deeply ingrained almost in the subconscious of an organization. This is a sort of an attitude at an organizational level. The attitude makes the organization conducive to acquisition, transfer, and creation of knowledge. It is essentially an enabler.

This attitude also represents a capability, an enabling capability. If it is an enabling capability, then it can be built by an organization through manipulation of its component factors. This capability would influence the manifest culture and innovation output of the organization. It will contribute to the overall innovation capability of the organization.

The Google story gives some clues on what it takes to build the right attitude. There seems to be a certain kind of openness in the organization. There is a keen awareness of what is happening in the world around them. As also there seems to be an almost playful experimentation that appears to exist at the core of their innovation design.

Attitudinal Capability

❀

In an earlier chapter of the book attitudinal capability has been defined as a relational asset (or an asset composed of emotional or attitudinal state of an organization), that acts as an enabler for creating new knowledge in a firm. There is a need to demystify this capability and how it helps create new knowledge as also figure out what organizations could do to build this capability. The creation of knowledge requires three distinct steps. The first is acquiring knowledge both from within and outside the organization. The second step is that of transferring it to locations where it is required. The final step is combining the available knowledge in a novel manner to create new knowledge that the organization can use to build efficiency, launch new products or services, expand markets or save cost.

Acquisition of knowledge in a continuous manner requires a certain attitude. The ability to look out into the environment, welcome new ideas and thoughts, and a questioning mind. Google's concept of identifying where their search technology could make a difference has helped them come up with varied applications like GMail, Google Desktop, Google Answers and of course, Google News. Combining various kinds of knowledge also takes a special attitude to knowledge itself. Seeing connections where none have existed till now and the ability to play one set of ideas with another set of ideas. Google has also used capabilities from different parts of itself to come up with new ideas. In October 2004, Google acquired Keyhole, a digital satellite image mapping company. Out of the Keyhole acquisition, came two very different applications. One is Google Earth, where users can zoom in on satellite images of any place in the world. The second, at the opposite end of the spectrum, is Google Local and Google Maps, that help users (in North America initially) to find navigation information and maps to any place that they wanted to get to.

This special attitude that Google has developed is clearly multidimensional. There are four distinct attitudinal attributes or factors that contribute to attitudinal capability.

Openness

Openness has been shown by management theorists to have a direct link with organizational learning.[1] The willingness to absorb new ideas, step out of comfort zones, trying out new ways of doing things, and comfort with often ambiguous and conflicting knowledge is broadly what openness is all about. This openness operates at many levels. The first level is an atmosphere of free exchange of ideas within an organization. People at all levels respecting ideas that other people come up with, results in a surfeit of important knowledge traveling across the organization. The key here is listening and absorbing.

The second level is about not getting caught in functional silos. Active and open collaboration without any hidden agendas on projects often results in breakthrough innovations. In a truly open organization this collaboration would happen both at a formal and informal levels. The third level of openness is about the willingness to experiment with new ideas that lie beyond the comfort zone of the organization. There is an element of risk-taking here. Backing radical projects takes a higher order of openness. This is because the organization is open to difficult projects as well as failure.

The final level is about being open to information or knowledge from outside organizational boundaries. Free flow of knowledge from outside the organization often creates discomfort. The reason behind that is

The Indian Angle—Tata Motors

When working on the Indica, Tata Motors had a massive challenge on their hands. The car was to be a completely indigenously developed car and more importantly, was to be value for money. This in an industry dominated by MNCs that had decades of passenger car experience and the budgets to match.

Tata didn't quite get it right the first time around. In 2001, with a poor quality car on its hands and a Rs 500 cr (5 bn) loss, the organization was probably at its lowest point ever. Ravi Kant, the managing director knew that drastic steps had to be taken and he took them.

Tata Motors realized, as an organization, they needed to be more open and listen to what the market was telling them. Tata Motors embarked on a knowledge exercise that took its suppliers right into their car. The organization began asking its suppliers not only to give them the best quality parts at the best value but also to join them in understanding what the parts did in the entire car—and how that entire car could be improved.

The insights that Tata Motors got out of this knowledge are extraordinary. This resulted in an entirely new and improved version of the Indica being launched. By 2005, not only did Tata Motors have 18% of the passenger car market, but they had also turned 2001's Rs 500 cr loss into a profit of Rs 1,237 cr. Tata Motors is clearly on a roll. A roll that began with a shift in their attitude. An attitude that called for more openness, awareness, and curiosity about the marketplace and its customers.

that this new knowledge may question the basic assumptions the organization operates on. Also, the information coming in may be contradictory. It takes a really open organization to be able to process and absorb this knowledge. Often this knowledge is what helps organizations create breakthrough innovation.[2] Keeping in sync with environment also results in a series of process and incremental innovations.

The organizations can play a significant role in building this attitude. For internal openness there needs to be a trusting environment in the organization. For external orientation there needs to be a value that the organization needs to place on external knowledge. Both Dupont and Shell place a significant value on external knowledge. In Dupont's University program they actively solicit research compounds by paying and partnering university researchers. At Shell's Game Changer too, they invite ideas from the general public and depending on who the idea comes from, either purchase information or materials, and/or invest in the organization.

IBM's Alphaworks puts its alpha software or initial level software on the Internet for outside software developers to play with. They let developers use the code, improve it, change it, and give feedback on it for a period of 90 days. IBM also lets developers use the code as base code for developing their own applications as well. This process has helped IBM fast-track their emerging technology development time to the market, from as much as 2–3 years to as little as six months.

Awareness

Any organization that wants to be innovating continuously has to be clued into the changes happening in the world around them. These changes could be social, technological, demographic or political. Discontinuities brought about by change represent new bases of knowledge. When knowledge of these discontinuities is combined with existing internal expertise, new knowledge or innovation happens. An aware organization is one that is always aware of its surroundings. These include customers, suppliers, immediate and wider society, and state of knowledge in various fields.

Within this overall construct of awareness is a higher order of awareness. This is the ability to abstract higher order concepts from the happenings in the world. This is the ability to see beyond events and be aware that events maybe connected in many ways. And if these connections are deciphered, new knowledge may emerge.

Awareness is a state that an innovative organization should strive to achieve. Placing value on this attitude should be at the core of the organization. People working in the organization themselves need to be made aware of the need to be aware of the world around them.

Curiosity

A constantly questioning attitude is certain to bring in knowledge. And questioning basic assumptions may bring in knowledge that has a major impact on the innovation process. Children in their learning years

Figure 4.1: Building Attitudinal Capability

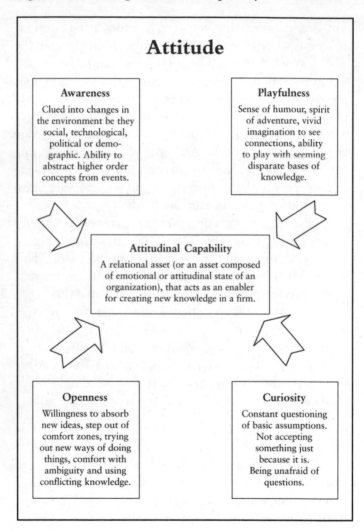

have this marvelous sense of curiosity. Their view of the world is full of wonder and the words they use most are "Why" and "How." This drives their phenomenal learning in the formative years. The greater the curiosity, the faster and better people learn.[3]

The same holds true for organizations. Asking questions is sure to bring in new knowledge that the organization needs to feed the innovation tunnel. This questioning attitude takes time and effort to develop. The organization should encourage challenging assumptions and the quest for knowledge.

There is another deeper side to curiosity. The knowledge or information that is available in the environment often is about phenomena that have happened in the past or are currently happening. There is hardly any insight into why they are happening the way they are. This is where curiosity steps in. Constantly asking "why" and "how" phenomena are taking place makes people aware of not only occurrences, but the probable reasons behind these occurrences. Knowing why phenomena happen the way they happen, is what insight is all about. These insights very often are unavailable to competitors. These can become significant sources of competitive advantage. Being curious can pay off in more ways than one.

Playfulness

This is the most important part of creating new knowledge or innovating. When faced with various kinds of knowledge, it takes a certain sense of humor, a spirit of adventure and vivid imagination to see connections among those various kinds of knowledge. When one is able to play these bases of knowledge against one another and establish some sort of connections, combining knowledge to create new knowledge becomes very easy. Combining knowledge in unexpected ways is the hallmark of good humor. Anyone who has ever tried to tell a good joke will know that the more unexpected the punch line, the better the joke will be received.

The same is true of creative ideas. The more unexpected the thought, the more interesting the idea is likely to be. Therefore, keeping an open mind will turn the mind more receptive to making new unexpected connections. One organization that keeps the humor quotient up is Southwest Airlines. Southwest has employees that make fake in-flight announcements, play dress-up and dance, and do just about anything to entertain passengers. Southwest is also one of the world's most profitable airlines, one that has been profitable from its second year of operation. Second year!

There really is something to Southwest's policy that people who have a good sense of humor tend to be more creative, more relaxed about life and, therefore more productive. Playfulness in general and humor more specifically is seen to have a strong relationship with reducing stress, improving inter-personal skills, fostering creativity, and driving rapid learning.[4] The humor–creativity link is important and can drive innovation. Southwest's playful attitude does not manifest itself only as fun and games. Employees at Southwest are empowered to make decisions to resolve any issue on hand. The airline also tracks the suggestions given by its employees. Southwest estimates that employee suggestions have saved them millions of dollars each year.

Sometimes serious contemplation is a hindrance in combining knowledge. A playful attitude makes the process more fun and results in novel combinations. Another thing that playfulness brings in is that the process of judgement is suspended for a while. In this suspension of judgement some really radical ideas that looked improbable at first maybe considered. It is a great way to come up with new ideas. Once the playful attitude has thrown up a large basket of ideas, they can be submitted to the rigorous process of the innovation tunnel.

Conclusion
❀

The manner in which an organization responds to stimuli is of great importance to the business of innovation. This automatic response depends on the attitude the organization possesses. It is extremely important to develop an attitude that is conducive to acquisition, transfer, processing, and creation of new knowledge. This attitude has to be at an organizational level. The development of this attitude takes time and effort and needs to be presented by the organization as a valued capability to have. Often corporate organizations tend to be hierarchical, humorless and formal. While some of them make token efforts at playfulness through activities run by the human resources department, very few organizations translate that playfulness into their daily working life. This lack of playfulness tends to destroy the attitude required for innovation to take place. While formal structures are required to run an organization efficiently, an open and often playful attitude is required for innovation.

Organizations that manage to bridge the efficient formal structure gap with attitudinal capability manage to be efficient and innovative at the same time. A variety of devices are used by the organizations to achieve this. Google's list of Top 100 priority projects at any given point in time actually has about 250 items on it, but the point is different. This active project list keeps the focus on things that are of interest to Google as an organization. Within this list, researchers choose what they are interested in and form teams that can get together for as little as a few weeks to many months to work on the ideas. While the formal structure of research teams is available, the openness of choosing your team because the project idea is of interest to you and disbanding once the project task is fulfilled keeps the organization playful and flexible enough to have maximum effectiveness.

Key Takeouts

❋

- Attitudinal capability is an important enabling capability that contributes to the overall innovation capability of an organization.
- The component factors of attitudinal capability are openness, awareness, curiosity and playfulness.
- These component factors help process knowledge, from acquisition to the creation of new knowledge.

Notes

1. Argyris, C. 1978. *Organizational Learning: A Theory of Action Perspective*. Reading, MA: Addison-Wesley Publishing Company; Senge, P.M. 1990. *The Fifth Discipline: The Art and Practice of the Learning Organization*. New York: Doubleday.
2. Leonard-Barton, D. 1992. Core Capabilities and Core Rigidities: A Paradox in Managing New Product Development. *Strategic Management Journal*, 13, Special Issue, 111–25.
3. Hensley, R.B. 2004. Curiosity and Creativity as Attributes of Information Literacy. *Reference and User Quarterly*, 44(1), 31–38.
4. Miller, J. 1996. Humor—An Empowerment Tool for the 1990s. *Empowerment in Organizations*, 4(2), 16–21.

Web Resources

1. http://www.google.com/corporate/business.html
2. http://www.google.com/corporate/tenthings.html
3. http://www.google.com/corporate/history.html
4. http://www.internet-story.com/google.htm
5. http://www.cbsnews.com/stories/2004/12/30/60minutes/main664063.shtml
6. http://www.businessweek.com/magazine/content/04_18/b3881001_mz001.htm
7. http://www.laughterremedy.com/humor.dir/humor11_00.html

8. http://btobsearch.barnesandnoble.com/booksearch/isbninquiry.asp?z=y&btob=Y&ean=9780767901840&displayonly=EXC
9. http://www.laughterremedy.com/articles/boost_creativity.html
10. http://rediff.co.in/money/2005/nov/19spec.htm
11. http://www.tata.com/tata_motors/articles/20040925_tata_motors.htm
12. http://knowledge.wharton.upenn.edu/index.cfm?fa=viewArticle&id=1275
13. http://www.tata.com/tata_motors/articles/20030802_crash_testing.htm
14. http://www.tata.com/tata_motors/articles/20030825_challenge.htm
15. http://www.tatamotors.com/our_world/press_releases.php?ID=227&action=Pull
16. http://www.tatamotors.com/our_world/press_releases.php?ID=192&action=Pull
17. http://www.tatamotors.com/our_world/research.php
18. http://domain-b.com/companies/companies_t/tcs/20041208_deal.html
19. http://www.tata.com/tata_motors/articles/20030424_rebuilding_success_stories.htm
20. http://www.cfoasia.com/archives/200512-01.htm

5 | Getting Creative

Creative Capability ❀ *Techniques*
❀ *Communication* ❀ *Innovation Space*
❀ *Conclusion* ❀ *Key Takeouts*

IBM has re-invented itself time and again over the last 95 years. Look at IBM's advertising today—the "helpdesk" campaign—does it look or feel like a 95 year old company? Certainly not. Few companies have willingly shed their heritage and glorious past like IBM. Yet for IBM, this is a time of renaissance. In the 1920s, it was a manufacturer of tabulating machines. In 1953, it entered the computer business and in the 1950s and 60s, became the largest manufacturer of mainframe and standalone computers in the world. The 1980s saw IBM transform itself into a PC manufacturer and move into the consumer space from a previously pure corporate space. Come the 21st century and IBM (though the initials stand for International Business

Machines), is largely a software and services company, having sold off its PC business to Lenovo. Through the decades, the IBM brand has been growing stronger. In 2004, it clocked record sales of US $96.5 billion and a record profit of US $8.4 billion.

How has IBM consistently re-invented itself to remain at the forefront of technological innovation? That IBM has been doing this for many decades is evidenced by its 4,500 research employees, more than 15,000 patents and five Nobel Prize winner researchers. In the 21st century, IBM is encouraging its employees to share their information and ideas and work on them for growth.

IBM recognizes its employees as innovators. The IBM website abounds with stories of individual inventors who have done IBM proud with their innovations. One thing that IBM is very clear about is that in the 20th century, it may have been easier to make break-through innovation in technology because so much of technology was yet unexplored. In the 21st century, it is far more difficult, because customers no longer embrace technology for technology's sake. They question and evaluate the technology for the value that it provides them. In this scenario, IBM ensures that its employees get together and think about the implications of technology, to think about where technology can make a difference. Online communities like ThinkPlace encourage employees to post ideas and suggestions about IBM's products and services. Many of them make it through to evaluation for commercial testing. It's not enough to merely set up the forum, it is necessary to encourage active participation as well.

In an era where most organizations are trying to block employee access to "goof-off" on the Internet where they perceive "random surfing" taking place, IBM has set up blogging communities where upwards of 3,000 employees actively blog about whatever that strikes them as interesting. While an exhaustive code of conduct exists about blogging behavior, the flip-side is that this code of conduct has been devised by the employees themselves through a "wiki" site—where changes can be made and viewed online. IBM bloggers include very senior IBM employees.

IBM encourages employees to think laterally about business problems or ideas while looking at the outside world. IBM even highlights inventors on their website and proudly talks about the results of their lateral thinking efforts. Llamas and auto insurance, computing grids and breast cancer, telematics and car problems, they all come together under IBM's initiative towards innovation and lateral thinking to get there.

But IBM is not creating communication spaces and thinking tools only for its employees. IBM also set up supply chain management curriculum at various US universities when it realized that business process problems would be the biggest area where IBM could see exponential growths. Not only is it focussing on an existing area of study like supply chain management, IBM is also developing a new area that it calls services science. IBM's services science combines anthropology, game theory and behavioral economics to integrate technology that makes services businesses more efficient and satisfying. IBM is working harder than ever to define the new face of technology in our world. That better than anything else answers the question in their new US ad campaign, "What makes you special?" IBM's answer, quite simply, is innovation.

Well, IBM seems to be doing interesting things in its quest for innovation. There are some techniques that they are using, lateral thinking for one. Other than that, they seem to be creating spaces where minds and streams of knowledge can meet and actively create new knowledge. Blogs and ThinkPlace are examples of this. Also, they seem to be creating forums for even new disciplines to deliberately let varying disparate streams mingle together to create competitive advantage through new knowledge. These set of things actually represent the third constituent capability that an organization can build. In the next section it is dealt with in detail.

Creative Capability
❀

Once an organization has built disparate reservoirs of knowledge and got its attitude absolutely right, one thing remains to be done, the onerous, very serious, playful and exciting task of combining these disparate bases of knowledge. Often this happens either by chance or by force of circumstance, or by a brilliant individual. All of these are not ideal for an organization that wants to deliver innovation continuously. Thus there is a need for a set of processes or assets in an organization that can make this combination of knowledge an ongoing process. In short, the organization needs creative capability.

Creative capability can be defined as the ability to bring together various types of knowledge in a novel manner. At times these stream would have to be brought together with some amount of force. If you banged the different streams together, the violent mix would create something new altogether. At other times the streams have to just mingle and create new forms of knowledge. There are a few time-tested ways of making this happen.

Techniques

Idea generation or generating options for the innovation tunnel is often seen as a black-box. Organizations employ a lot of tactics to get ideas without opening this black-box. The most popular among these tactics are brainstorming, putting up of idea bins and running contests. These tactics do not systematically bring together knowledge to create new knowledge or new ideas, or innovation in short.

In the IBM example in the beginning of the chapter there was the use of lateral thinking techniques invented by Edward de Bono.[1] The techniques used in lateral thinking essentially work by making novel combinations of existing knowledge or by inducing a type of knowledge that has not been considered before. Some of the techniques like "random insertion" in lateral thinking use a random object as a start point to start recombining knowledge that exists. The same holds true for "reversal" where the conventional wisdom is reversed. The most famous example of the use of this technique is the Indian cooking oil brand Saffola. Use of excess oil in cooking is supposed to be bad for the heart. But once the proposition was reversed to cooking oil that is good for the heart, existing knowledge about human health and certain vegetable oils could be recombined to deliver a breakthrough product.

Another interesting way to combine knowledge is the use of metaphors or metaphorical thinking. This technique has been used by a wide variety of people from religious leaders, to writers, and even organizations. The basic idea here is to force a metaphor and all that it represents onto an existing base of knowledge and then recombine knowledge in novel ways.

There are many other techniques that exist for creativity.[2] Any organization should make sure that these are spread through the organizations and become standard tools. This may be done through training programs, insistence on the fact that each idea be backed by use of techniques, etc.

Figure 5.1: Building Creative Capability

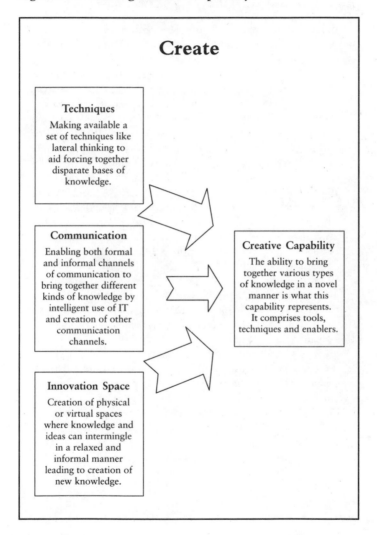

The Indian Angle—Biocon

Biocon, as one of India's largest biotechnology companies, has several active R&D projects at any given point in time. Started in 1978 by a lady who would eventually, if rather briefly, become India's richest woman, Kiran Mazumdar Shaw, Biocon focussed on generic pharmaceuticals. Generics was a field where more Indian pharma and biotech companies operated, with non-infringing manufacturing processes of patented drugs, or off-patent drugs.

However, the pharmaceutical industry is extremely competitive and any organization with an eye on the long-term like Biocon needed to look further up the value chain. Biocon recently ventured into collaborative R&D working with other organizations jointly on projects and sharing knowledge and results. Some of these projects require collaboration with teams in other countries; some require compliance to procedural norms like ISO 9001. Biocon needed to invest in R&D, which it did, increasing R&D investment by 76% in 2005 over 2004. However, Biocon also realized that to generate the maximum returns on their investment they had to make sure their teams worked to their maximum effectiveness. For this they needed the help of technology.

Biocon worked with IBM to create platforms to help its teams work and communicate better. These platforms ensured that the teams had ready access to norms and to each other. Using these platforms, Biocon's IT team then developed monitoring tools to help their scientists. The Laboratory Information Management Systems (LIMS) ensures that the outcome of clinical trials is directly updated on the system. This system can then be accessed not only by Biocon scientists but also their partner collaborators in other locations.

contd.

contd.

Biocon, therefore, has used technology to create a space for its scientific teams to communicate with each other and working towards the same goals on projects. Biocon has used technology to build its creative capability in an intensely scientific environment.

Communication

The techniques that were just discussed forced knowledge together in new ways almost like a particle collider. However, there are ways in which knowledge can be allowed to mingle in more benign ways. This approach is more continuous than episodic. Effective communication across levels and functions allow for mingling of ideas and knowledge in a seamless manner. Any organization that is serious about innovations needs to closely look at the robustness of communication.[3]

People within organizations communicate at two levels, formal and informal. The formal processes are often very well defined. But often they follow functional and hierarchical path flows. Not an ideal condition for an open sharing of ideas. Informal communication is often viewed with suspicion and discouraged. However, informal communication is probably the fastest way to exchange ideas. Communication with or just surfing of the outside world is also discouraged except for specific projects. This discourages flow of knowledge into the organization.

IBM may today be an organization that has got its game together in terms of innovation and its direction for the future. However, things were not always so great at the Big Blue. In the 1970s IBM believed that computers were just what its name meant—'Business Machines.' IBM had focused its entire product development process on making bigger and bigger machines that could handle massive computational tasks.

Meanwhile, however, two unlikely heroes by the names of Steve Jobs and Steve Wozniak were busy creat-ing the product that would create history—the Personal Computer (PC). The PC brought computing to every home and to every person's fingertips. By 1981, IBM had created its own PC—with an operating system called DOS from a tiny start-up called Microsoft. The IBM PC and Microsoft would soon become ubiquitous with the PC. And yet, once again, just like the previous years when IBM created an advantage for itself, opportunities passed IBM by. A lack of communication with each other and their customers meant that IBM once again lost its way in the competitive marketplace.

It was not until 1993 with the advent of Lou Gerstner Jr, that IBM once again began to pick up the pieces. They began again to talk to their customers and understand where the market was leading. And this time they correctly identified the movement as being towards the Internet and e-commerce. IBM now became the organization that helped other companies communicate.

Information technology is transforming the whole mode of communication within and outside organizations. Instant messengers, emails, bulletin boards, etc. can be great means of communication. P&G's MyINet posts ideas, information and experts for researchers to gather information, or have their research problems discussed/evaluated. The whole exchange of ideas can be accelerated by putting in place novel means of communication. Once ideas and knowledge are allowed to mingle, new knowledge is sure to blossom.

Innovation Space

Water coolers and coffee-vending machines are supposed to be the most productive places in an organization as far as coming up with innovative ideas is concerned. They bring people from various functions together in a rather relaxed and informal environment. Nobody is judging what is being said, and bingo! there is a flow of ideas. Can this be recreated in a deliberate manner to get a flow on innovative ideas?

IBM has created a virtual innovation space in the form of ThinkPlace. This is again a way of using information technology in an innovative manner. Organizations can create these virtual spaces through the use of intranet, like P&G's MyINet. Blogging sites also represent spaces where disparate bases of knowledge can be brought together.

Physical spaces can also be created in forms of creative lounges, meeting places and other spaces where knowledge can be brought together in pursuit of innovation.[4] 3M's Tech Forums are exactly these kind of open meetings where researchers get together to discuss their projects, ideas, and learn from each other's work. Special interests groups or committees, or hobby groups that relate to business innovation can also be created and can be a part of the whole innovation space that an organization possesses.

Conclusion
❋

The creative capability is the final step in formation of innovation capability of the organization. This is the capability that ensures output of ideas. The one thing that is important to note is that each of the three capabilities play a distinct role in making an organization deliver continuous innovation. Creative capability is a capability that works best if the other two capabilities—knowledge and attitudinal are well developed.

The effort in the creative capability is to create some amount of mingling as well as forcing together of different bases of knowledge. The accent is on doing it deliberately. This would create some amount of flux in the organization, which gets taken care of by the inherent attitudinal capability that the organization develops. The knowledge capability forms the bedrock of all this. In the next few chapters, development, maintenance and renewal of these capabilities would be dealt with in some amount of detail.

Key Takeouts
❋

- Knowledge residing in different parts of the organization and different individuals needs to be brought together to create new knowledge.
- Creative capability plays the role of bringing knowledge together.
- Constituents of creative capability are techniques, communication and innovation space.

Notes

1. De Bono, E. 1977. *Lateral Thinking*. Harmondsworth: Penguin Books.
2. Alder, H. 1994. The Technology of Creativity. *Management Decision*, 32(4), 23–29; Tanner, D. 1992. Applying Creative Thinking Techniques to Everyday Problems. *The Journal of Consumer Marketing*, 9(4), 23–28; McFadzen, E. 2000. Techniques to Enhance Creative Thinking. *Team Performance Management*, 6(3/4), 62–72.
3. Burns, T. and G.M. Stalker. 1961. *The Management of Innovation*. Oxford: Oxford University Press; Brown, S. and K.M. Eisenhardt. 1995. Product Development: Past Research, Present Findings and Future Directions. *Academy of Management Review*, 20(2), 343–78; Brown, S.L. and K.M. Eisenhardt. 1997. Art of Continuous Change: Linking Complexity Theory and Time Paced Evolution in Relentlessly Shifting Organizations. *Administrative Science Quarterly*, 42(1), 1–34.

4. Syrett, M. and J. Lammiman. 2002. *Successful Innovation*. London: Profile Books Ltd.

Web Resources

1. http://news.com.com/IBM+The+next+big+thing+no+longer+exists/2100-1008_3-6050056.html
2. http://www.pc.ibm.com/store/news/500_011304.html
3. http://domino.watson.ibm.com/comm/research.nsf/pages/d.math.cliff_pickover.html
4. http://www-03.ibm.com/developerworks/blogs/page/jasnell?entry=blogging_ibm
5. https://www-927.ibm.com/ibm/cas/cascon/workshopsignup/displayWorkshop?PublicView=true&Slot=WEDPM&Num=4
6. http://www-03.ibm.com/ibm/history/history/history_intro.html
7. http://news.com.com/IBM+Research+turns+60/2100-11395_3-5892661.html?tag=nl
8. http://news.com.com/IBMs+service+science/2010-1008_3-5201792.html?tag=st.rc.targ_mb
9. http://www-8.ibm.com/in/casestudies-sw/case_biocon.html

6 | Building Blocks

Individual ❀ *Team* ❀ *Organization*
❀ *Conclusion*
❀ *Key Takeouts*

In the last few chapters, the entire model of what innovation capability entails comes together. The challenge that remains is to build this capability at multiple levels[1] in the organization. If the elements of this capability are put in place across various levels in the organization then there is a good chance that it will become a part of the organizational fabric. Till now, the discussion has been at the overall organizational level. This chapter would take a more fine-grained view of innovation capability.

Any organization is composed of a set of people. These people are the driving force behind organizational activities. They take decisions, drive execution, contribute to strategy, and are made to face ambiguous situations almost everyday. Any firm or organization that aspires to be truly innovative should have people with ability to innovate in a continuous manner. Most of these innovations may at best be incremental, but they would contribute to the organization performing effectively. Also, if there is a wide base of capable people, the chances of scoring a breakthrough would be high.

People do not form the organization straightaway. They are usually organized in teams. These teams get the actual work done by bringing together individual capabilities. These teams themselves need to be able to build together the constituent capabilities of innovation capability to deliver continuous innovations. These capabilities have to be consciously built. It is not enough to just form teams. It is essential to enable and empower them with capabilities necessary to deliver innovative solutions.

Thus at the very minimum, there are three distinct levels at which innovation capability is required to be built. Starting with individuals, then teams, and finally at the overall organizational level.

Individual

❀

An individual who wants to be innovative or creative or has the ability to come up with ideas continuously also needs to follow the path suggested for building innovation capability in organizations as a whole.

The individual needs to be aware of a large body of knowledge or better still, bodies of knowledge. This person should have the right tools/techniques and the right attitude.

An individual's knowledge capability is to some extent determined by the background, the education, and the interests the person has. If the person has had an education that has given him exposure to a wide variety of subjects, has a range of interests and is well traveled, then the person would be well equipped to produce new knowledge. Some of the most well known inventors and innovators fit this profile. Historically, however, prolific inventors like Edison, Einstein and Leonardo Da Vinci were self-taught; learning about subjects that interested them with a voracious appetite to learn more. Da Vinci taught himself anatomy, architecture, created the first prototype for a robot, and the first design for a flying machine. And he is most famous for a painting! Inventors like Da Vinci then worked to apply that learning into practical experiments and applications, with a love of discovery.

The organization can make a huge impact as well on the knowledge capability of an individual. The key to this is to provide exposure to the individual both within and outside the organization. Within the organization, initiatives like role rotation, multifaceted training and multi-skilling would help. Placement out of the organization for sometime, either for higher education or specific training would also help.

Attitudinal capability requires some amount of training. The values of dimensions of openness, awareness, curiosity and playfulness are not easy to cultivate in an organization. At a children's playground certainly, but in an office, somehow, people seem to leave all these qualities behind. However, a bigger impact can be made if these values are part of the social fabric of the organization. That would ensure that individuals value these and apply them in their work life. Providing people with some amount of autonomy as far as work is concerned would also make people more open and aware. This is because with autonomy comes responsibility, and the need to be open to and aware of the environment.

Employees need to possess a full toolkit as far as techniques for combining knowledge are concerned. They should be exposed to everything from lateral thinking to metaphorical thinking. This calls for extensive training of individuals and well as opportunities to practice and hone these skills. Of course, as with any training, the employee needs to see value in the program and see that the organization places importance on the practice of that training.

The key idea here is to take a systematic approach to creation of new ideas or innovation at an individual level. Often being innovative is taken as a personality trait. This is not correct to a large extent. Innovation capability at an individual level can be built pretty systematically.

Table 6.1: Building Blocks of Innovation Capability

	Individual	Team	Organization
Knowledge capability	Role rotation, Multi-skilling, Multifaceted training	Team diversity, Social capital, Communities of practice	Workforce diversity, Systems, R&D, Social capital
Creative capability	Techniques	Creative tension, Facilitation	Process, Systems, Structure
Attitudinal capability	Autonomy, Training	Facilitation, Team identity	Structure, Shared values

Team

A team is essentially a group of individuals involved in a set of tasks that have a common goal. At this level, the ways and means of developing innovation capability are quite different from an individual level. The individual capabilities would have to be harnessed here to build a capability that is bigger than the sum of individual capabilities. P&G has a formal process to put together research teams. P&G creates a team that has a combination of an older, experienced person and a younger person for energy and enthusiasm. The team will also have a combination of domain knowledge and "translation expertize." Translation expertise is the kind of experience that comes with being able to translate technical output into user-friendly applications. P&G also makes this team work literally together. Even if initially the team is from different locations or countries, in putting together a specialized team, P&G will ensure that the team works in close spaces, next to each other, to keep up the spirit of enthusiasm.

Knowledge capability of a team can be maximized at the selection stage itself. Members of a team should have diversity in the expertise they bring to the table. If the team is homogeneous then there will be a great degree of comfort, but the knowledge base will be narrow. Diversity in a team is a must if creation of new knowledge is the objective. The two other things that can increase the knowledge base are the connections that the team members have with the outside world, as well as the strength of relationships within the team. This is the notion of group social capital,[2] where knowledge is the resource embedded in relationships.

The attitude that a team possesses needs to be developed as a part of team identity. The teams need to learn that a certain attitude is required to be able to innovate continuously. The team needs to identify with the attitudinal dimensions and inculcate it into its work processes and interactions. Attitude is something that only develops over a period of time and requires sustained effort. Facilitation from trained team behavior experts in the initial phases may well play an important role.

At a team level, while techniques are important for creative capability, a greater role is played by team processes and systems. Effective communication has to be ensured to make sure that knowledge is exchanged and creation of new knowledge becomes possible. Apart from this, teams may require facilitation to ensure informal exchange of knowledge. Information technology can also be exploited at a team level for effective communication and for creating innovation space.

Building innovation capability at a team level is a little more complex than building it at an individual level. Teams are entities where most of the organization's work gets done. Usually teams engage in collaborative problem-solving, which is essentially creation of new knowledge. Thus it becomes important to build capabilities at the team level.

Organization
❀

The organization level building of innovation capability has been extensively dealt with in the earlier chapters. There are a few things that can happen only at the organization level. These are specifically investments in R&D and market research that build knowledge capability. These have to be driven from organizational imperatives. At an organizational level it is necessary to put systems and processes in place that drive some of the imperatives of building innovation capability. Thus systems and processes are needed to build workforce diversity, provide multifaceted training, and build communication channels. This is true across capabilities. The organization structure also needs to be tinkered to build some of these capabilities.

At an overall level, a strong sense of shared values is required to build the right attitude. This is something again that can be tackled only at an organization level and has impact on the team as well as individual levels.

Conclusion
❋

The right approach to innovation capability is a multi-level approach. What this approach does is that it makes the capability really robust. It no longer remains only an organizational aspiration. Rather it touches each individual and every work team, and eventually the organization. There is no escape from this multi-level approach. Innovation can become embedded in the fabric of an organization only if it is incorporated at all levels. Individuals who are high on innovation capability can contribute both to teams and organization as a whole effectively.

However, having capable individuals is just not enough. When teams are formed then a new set of challenges crop up. On especially challenging projects, for example, a certain diversity in team composition would be required, so that all knowledge areas that are required for problem solving are covered. As also, enabling mechanism to aid knowledge combination would be required. So having capable individuals alone would not lead to effective teams. Putting in place mechanisms that build team innovation capability contribute to the overall innovativeness of an organization.

Certain things can only be done at an organizational level. Overall policy direction is always determined at the organizational level; values and beliefs contributing to attitudinal capability can be effectively set only at an organization level. Thus organizational level initiatives also become extremely important.

This also means that a fragmented approach to building this capability may not be very successful. The organization that will be most successful in implementing this will take an integrated approach. This capability would also be long lasting if an integrated approach is taken so that the constituent capabilities are deeply embedded in the organization.

Key Takeouts

✤

- A multi-level approach to building innovation capability is required.
- Constituent capabilities need to be built at the levels of individual, team and organization.
- Only an integrated approach will maximize benefits to the organization.

Notes

1. Drazin, R., M.A. Glynn and R.K. Kazanjian. 1999. Multilevel Theorizing about Creativity in Organizations: A Sensemaking Perspective. *Academy of Management Review*, 24(2), 286–307.
2. Oh, H., M. Chung and L. Giuseppe. 2004. Group Social Capital and Group Effectiveness: The Role of Informal Socializing Ties. *Academy of Management Journal*, 47(6), 860–75.

Web Resource

1. http://www.fastcompany.com/articles/2001/08/pg2.html

7 | Staying the Course

Vision ❀ Goals ❀ Shared Values ❀ Systems and Processes ❀ Outcome/Output Measurement ❀ Learning and Feedback ❀ Conclusion ❀ Key Takeouts

In the last chapter it was argued that to be successful with building innovation capability, a multi-level approach has to be followed. Building capabilities at multiple levels also ensures their longevity to some extent. Extending this argument in this chapter, a close look is taken at how to make sure that these capabilities are long lasting. A lot of organizational initiatives turn out to be temporary fads. They are touted as the solution to all problems and then rolled out. However, they fizzle out pretty soon. This creates disillusionment and disappointment within the organization. The reason for this is that often there are no visible results from these short-lived initiatives. Such results could lead to the organization members treating all initiatives with distrust. For any initiative to be successful, the organization needs to develop trust in its ability to deliver results.

Any change that an organization wants to introduce has to be persisted with for a significant period of time. Building lasting innovation capability would require a systematic effort over a period of time. These days often, results are sought instantly. There is nothing wrong with this attitude per se, but what has to be understood is that capabilities are like infrastructure that take time to build and give benefits over long periods of time.

This can happen only if there is an effort to make any initiative an integral part of the organizational architecture. The vision, goals, systems, processes and values of the organization that essentially form its architecture should reflect the priorities brought about by the need to build innovation capability. Unless these set of architectural elements reflect innovation priorities, the organization as a whole would not take seriously the need to build innovation capability.

Measuring something ensures focus on what is being measured. A lot of organizational priorities are a result of what is measured. If market share is measured it tends to become one of the important performance parameters. Hence for an innovation capability initiative to succeed, important innovation capability led outcomes and ouputs should be measured. The quantified results then need to be analysed for the learning to be fed back into the organization (see Figure 7.1). Only such a systematic process would result in building lasting capabilities.

Vision
❀

The vision of an organization represents its long-term aspirations.[1] This is usually put together as an inspirational statement that binds the organization together. A lot of innovative organizations have innovation built into their vision statements. IBM's values at work statements include that IBMers' actions will be driven by "Innovation that matters, for the company and for the world." 3M's industrial tapes and adhesives segment has a vision that states "To be recognized as an innovative solutions provider by every customer that we serve".

Vision is something that guides an organization over a significant period of time. It is like a guidepost that always keeps the organizational efforts focused in one direction. This makes vision extremely important. Any organizational aspiration that is seen as important should form a part of the vision. This will ensure that the particular aspiration stays visible. This essentially means that organizations that are serious about having long lasting innovation capability have to build it

Figure 7.1: Building Lasting Capabilities

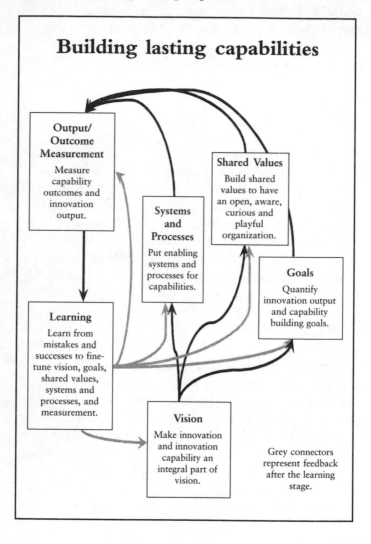

into their vision. How they do it depends on the context in which they operate. But it has to be built in very strongly.

Also given that vision is later broken down into goals, systems/processes and shared values, it becomes the driver of what happens in an organization everyday.

Goals
❀

Vision translates into goals that drive the organization in the medium term. The goals have to represent the priorities set out by the vision. These goals have to be measurable so as to monitor them over time. Organizations usually put goals in terms of revenue, profit, and market share. However, if innovation is a priority then the goals need to also have the innovation component built into them. The typical goal built around innovation is that a certain percentage of sales need to be from new products/innovation developed within the last five year span. For P&G, that percentage is more than 35%, for Dupont that percentage is currently at 33%.

Specifically in case of innovation capability, not only goals for innovation output (usually defined in terms of new products, services, percentage of business from NPD, etc.) but also outcome goals for constituent capabilities become important. Outcome measurements for each of the three capabilities, knowledge, attitudinal and creative, have to be done. These should become the part of the goal sheet of each and every part of the organization. Only then the development of innovation capability will happen in a focused manner in the organization.

Shared Values
❊

Attitudinal dimensions of openness, awareness, curiosity and playfulness are extremely important to innovation capability. These have to become a part of the shared value system to then become organizational attitude. A strong program of shared values has to be put in place by the organization to develop attitude conducive to innovation capability. A shared value program has to do with more than just attitudinal development. The emphasis has to be on a culture of innovation, placing value on knowledge and developing the right attitude.

Shared values, in short, have to become a part of organizational architecture. These values then shape the culture of the organization. Values and beliefs are at the base of this culture. Very simply, if the organization wants to have a strong "innovation culture", shared values of openness, awareness, curiosity and playfulness become fundamental.

Systems and Processes

✻

Strong systems and processes are required in two of the capabilities that contribute to overall innovation capability. Knowledge capability requires strong systems and processes to be able to recruit a diverse workforce, conduct robust market research, have successful R&D, and give multifaceted training. What should be appreciated here is that building these systems is often a multifunctional exercise. Multiple departments are involved simultaneously. For example, a diverse workforce and training involve the human resource functions as well as other functions where these initiatives take place. Only if strong systems and processes exist would these dimensions of knowledge capability be delivered in a consistent manner.

Similarly, the communication dimension of creative capability needs strong systems and processes to facilitate both formal and informal communication that lead to creation of new knowledge. A lot of organizations are using strong IT systems to build these systems and processes. IT in fact, can enable both formal and informal communication. The organization needs to build these systems and processes in a robust manner, so that they become an integral part of the organizational architecture. They will, in turn, provide long lasting innovation capability.

Outcome/Output Measurement

❈

It is very important to measure both outcomes and output. Usually the very act of measurement by the organization is taken as a signal by organizational members. Whatever is being measured becomes important to deliver, especially if rewards are attached to such a measurement. Thus it is very important to measure whatever is being driven through the organization. In the case of innovation capability, the outcomes that come out of each of the constituent capabilities need to be measured as well as the innovation output. When A.G. Lafley became the CEO of P&G in 2000, the organization had a less than 35% success rate of new innovations that went to market. Lafley knew that if this rate had to improve, then P&G needed broader and richer sources of innovation. Thus, was born the P&G diktat that the inspiration or roots of 50% of P&G's innovation had to come from external sources. It has worked—in six years R&D productivity has increased by 60%, while R&D costs have dropped from 4.8% of sales to 3.5%.

The other benefit that comes out of measurement is course correction. Measurement provides a sense of what is working and what is not working. This allows to course correct some of the initiatives. This could determine the long term success of any initiative.

Learning and Feedback

❀

The data results of measuring output and outcome provide important learning in terms of what is working and what is not working. This learning then has to be fed back into the starting point of this entire process. The vision may require clarification. One is not suggesting a frequent revamp of vision. But it may need more clarity to help define the rest of the process.

Similarly, goals may have to be fine-tuned. Systems and processes may have to be strengthened or altered. And shared values might have to be approached in a completely new manner. Using feedback properly would result in the strengthening of innovation capability in the organization. This process has to be robust and followed rigorously.

Conclusion

❀

Staying the course is important in any initiative, especially when it involves building long lasting capabilities that would contribute to the innovation capability of an organization. Putting an overall organizational architecture in place is the most important thing that an organization can do to make the said capabilities relatively permanent. A strong vision that incorporates innovation priorities is the first step in putting this architecture in place. This vision should then lead to focused, measurable goals, robust systems and processes, and a strong set of shared values. These have to be persevered with to an extent over a period of time so that they can have a measurable impact.

Equally important is course correction based on feedback. Each organization operates in a unique context. The context would make some components work better than others. Key output/outcome parameters should be measured to figure out what is working and what is not working. Then adjustments have to be made in every cycle to keep the capabilities relevant.

Organizations can build long lasting capabilities only if they show a judicious mix of resilience and flexibility.

Key Takeouts
❋

- Building lasting innovation capability takes a systematic approach.
- Vision of the organization should incorporate innovation priorities.
- A strong organizational architecture comprising shared values, systems and processes, and goals is needed.
- Measurement and feedback are important to keep the system robust.

Note

1. Hatch, M.J. and M.S. Schultz. 2001. Are the Strategic Stars Aligned for Your Corporate Brand? *Harvard Business Review*, February, 128–34.

Web Resource

1. http://media.corporate-ir.net/media_files/irol/73/73320/Databook_2005.pdf

8 | Renew

Knowledge Capability
❋ *Attitudinal Capability* ❋
Creative Capability ❋ *Conclusion*
❋ *Key Takeouts*

The passage of time does a lot of stuff that may not be visible in the short term, especially with regard to capabilities that are represented by organizational processes and assets. There is a need to stay current as far as these capabilities are concerned or they will represent no competitive advantage at all. In the first instance, it might pay to look at what are the factors that impact these capabilities.

First, the environment itself is dynamic. It is in the nature of the environment to evolve in which an organization operates. There are various parts of an environment—legal, institutional, social, competition, partners, customers, etc. All of these undergo changes over a period of time. There is a need for organizations to build capabilities that are in sync with these changes or can track along with these changes. A simple example is the assumption that a mass marketing company may have about its consumers. Social mores and norms keep changing and it results in a change in the values and beliefs of consumers. Being out of sync with this change can be catastrophic. The consumer based knowledge should essentially be constantly updated.

Something quite different happens within organizations. It is easy for organizations to fall into predictable routines irrespective of the environment. It provides freedom from ambiguity and a sense of comfort. Set routines also provide efficiency in the near term. This can be dangerous in face of a changing environment. A changing environment can result in some of these routines being anachronistic and counterproductive. Hindustan Motors was comfortable churning out its ancient Ambassadors year on after year on. When the Indian market opened up and international manufacturers entered with their more advanced cars, consumers abandoned the Ambassador without a second thought. Hindustan Motors was left holding the bucket with over 11,000 employees to manufacture a mere 18,000 Ambassadors in 2002.

Organizations usually bureaucratize over a period of time in their quest for efficiency.[1] Rigidity in communication procedures is usually the result of this bureaucracy. Rules and procedures tend to dominate. Hierarchy becomes an overriding feature. This provides for greater control and coordination but destroys the elements required for continuous innovation.

Finally, there is no capability that is absolute. To have a competitive advantage the capabilities that you possess should be superior to the ones that your immediate competitors possess. Otherwise, these capabilities are of little advantage. This relative measure in terms of capabilities is very important.

P&G competes in a cut-throat sphere of business where they are squeezed from every side of the supply chain. Their consumers, customers, and trade are all looking for better and better deals every year. P&G itself has to keep improving its performance every year. And this in an industry that represents fast-moving consumer goods. The FMCG industry is one that sees a maximum number of product launches and variants in a year and for P&G to keep pace and continue to be the leader is something that reflects P&G's competitive capabilities. P&G's competition is other large corporations like itself, small local/regional players, and even store brands. P&G needs to out-innovate all these people and it does so by ensuring it has better market/consumer knowledge, and makes better use of it.

The three constituent capabilities of innovation capability are also susceptible to these forces. There is a need to constantly renew them, to keep them relevant. The ability to keep them fresh and germane would have a bearing on the long-term competitiveness of any firm.

Knowledge Capability

✱

Knowledge is a dynamic resource. The content as well as the quantity of knowledge in the world keeps changing. In fact, the quantity of information only keeps increasing. A simple search for the word "innovation" on Google yields 827 million results. The word "sex" on the other hand, just gives us 750 million results. This says something about the proliferation of knowledge in the area of innovation alone.

It also says something about the knowledge capability of the organization. The problem lies in staying current with the changes in the content of knowledge as well as having a good idea about areas of knowledge that maybe needed to drive the organization forward. If these are not updated, then there is a chance that the reservoir of knowledge in the organization would become archaic.

The environment is also fairly dynamic. The institutions, legal framework, customers, etc. undergo significant changes over periods of time. This knowledge is critical to make new combinations of knowledge. Again, keeping pace with such changes is important. The knowledge about the context or the environment has often resulted in breakthrough innovations when this knowledge has been combined with technical knowledge. As women became more and more active, with lives outside the house, feminine hygiene technology had to but keep pace. P&G's research on polyethylene fibers and absorption led to the launch of the Always/Whisper franchise in 1983.

Another important bit about knowledge capability is that when compared to competitors, this capability should be at a higher level. Any organization that aims to compete should strive to hold the kind of knowledge that the competition does not possess. This knowledge would then help the organization surprise competition with new innovations. However, if in an organization this capability is not constantly renewed it may fall behind competition.

Table 8.1: Impact of Time Variable on Knowledge Capability

	Change brought about by the time variable	Renewal strategy
Knowledge capability	Knowledge currently held by the organization becomes outdated. Assumptions about the context change drastically. Competitors discover new fields of knowledge that give them an edge.	Constantly scan for changes in the environment; knowledge held internally should always be in sync with the environment.

The organization that wants to keep its knowledge capability constantly renewed has to scan the environment constantly. The scanning has to determine any changes that might take place in the environment that would have an impact on the relevance of its own knowledge capability. A scanning function in the organization is therefore essential.

Once the changes are known, the organization can tweak the components of knowledge capability to suit its requirements. It can hire individuals who possess the specialist knowledge it requires. The R&D function can be reoriented and redirected to gather new knowledge. New networks and alliances can be formed. Google researchers make new teams depending on the research task on hand. P&G also creates R&D teams on the basis of the expertise and knowledge required. Training can also take up the new objective of constant updating of knowledge in the organization.

Attitudinal Capability
❋

Internal organizational processes can wreak havoc on this particular capability. In particular, there is a tendency for organizations to become bureaucracies. This is often done in the pursuance of greater efficiency and exercise of greater control. Rigid rules and procedures become part of the organizational architecture. Deviance from laid down rules often invites censure. Communication is strictly done through hierarchical channels.

Even after the organization has expended time and effort to inculcate openness, awareness, curiosity and playfulness, it needs to constantly watch out for bureaucratizing tendencies. Nature of attitude that needs to be inculcated in the organization changes over time. What represented openness a few decades ago is just par for the course in today's context. The components need to be redefined in the changing context continuously.

If an organization has been successful in its endeavors over some period of time then it shifts into a comfort zone. There is then a tendency to look inwards. This reduces awareness of the outside world. Even the need to question diminishes. Success can put an organization into an attitudinal slumber.

Table 8.2: Impact of Time Variable on Attitudinal Capability

	Change brought about by the time variable	Renewal strategy
Attitudinal capability	Hierarchy tends to take over. Processes that fostered attitude themselves become rigid and are taken for granted. Over time there is a tendency to look inwards. Tendency to question reduces as organization hits a comfort zone.	Keep auditing the attitude and discover fresh ways to drive it.

The one thing that any organization has to keep doing is have some understanding of where it stands in terms of attitudinal capability. This capability is relational, and deals with elusive elements like attitude and emotional states, which makes it difficult to monitor. Regular audits maybe called for to be able to track it. The results of the audit will provide directions for renewal. Usually fresh approaches and ideas will keep this capability renewed.

Creative Capability
❊

Changing tools, techniques and technology impact this capability over a period of time. Communication is increasingly dependent on technology and to make sure that the organization stays at the cutting edge of communication, relevant technologies have to be tracked and adopted. Some of the best tools of collaboration like instant messenger and blogging have had mixed reception as far as the corporate world is concerned. However, smart innovating companies have exploited them to their advantage. Staying ahead in terms of communication ensures that the organization is at the forefront of creating new knowledge.

Table 8.3: Impact of Time Variable on Creative Capability

	Change brought about by the time variable	Renewal strategy
Creative capability	New and better ways of communicating. New possibilities for creating innovating communities. Advanced techniques for combining knowledge.	Stay current with techniques and technologies.

Technology also plays a role in creating innovation space in new and unique ways. Again, it pays to keep looking at new innovations that would aid the creation of new knowledge. Anything from architecture that creates physical spaces to IT that can create virtual spaces, would have to be tracked.

There is a lot of research that takes place in terms of creativity techniques around the world. New ways of forcing disparate kinds of knowledge are devised. These again, if tracked and used early, can confer a distinct competitive advantage.

Conclusion
❋

It is not enough to just build capabilities once and then forget about them. They will only represent a strong competitive advantage if they are relevant in a changing context. Any capability is a prisoner of the context it operates in. Change the environment and the capability may not work so well. This is true for innovation capability as well.

Various parts of the environment change over a period of time. A change in societal context results in consumer behavior undergoing a change. Technology change brings in new ways of doing things. Institutional environment may result in new laws that make understanding of new knowledge bases very important. In the past couple of decades, environmental law has had a huge impact on how companies do business.

Organizations themselves change becoming rigid and routine bound. This means that they have to watch out and renew continuously to maintain good attitudinal and creative capabilities.

In short, innovation capability has to be renewed constantly. As an extension, its component capabilities also have to be renewed.

Key Takeouts
❋

- Environment is constantly changing and may make capabilities outdated.
- Organizations have a tendency for bureaucratization.
- Competitors develop their own capabilities over time, and the challenge is to stay ahead of them.
- Constant renewal of capabilities is required to keep them as a source of competitive advantage.

Note

1. Burns, T. and G.M. Stalker. 1961. *The Management of Innovation*. Oxford: Oxford University Press.

Web Resource

1. http://www.aworldconnected.org/article.php/301.html

Bibliography

❋

Argyris, C. 1978. *Organizational Learning: A Theory of Action Perspective*. Reading, MA: Addison-Wesley Publishing Company.

Burns, T. and G.M. Stalker. 1961. *The Management of Innovation*. Oxford: Oxford University Press.

Davila, T., M.J. Epstein and R. Shelton. 2006. *Making Innovation Work*. New Jersey: Wharton School Publishing.

De Bono, E. 1977. *Lateral Thinking*. Harmondsworth: Penguin Books.

Decker, C.L. 1998. *Winning with the P&G 99: 99 Principles and Practices of Procter and Gamble's Success*. London: HarperBusiness.

Doug, G. 1999. *IBM Redux: Lou Gerstner and the Business Turnaround of the Decade*. New York: HarperBusiness.

Freiberg, K. and J. Freiberg. 1997. *Nuts!: Southwest Airlines' Crazy Recipe for Business and Personal Success*. New York: Broadway Books.

Friedman, T. 2005. *The World is Flat: A Brief History of Globalized World in the 21st Century*. London: Penguin Books.

Ghoshal, S. and C.A. Bartlett. 1997. *The Individualized Corporation: A Fundamentally New Approach to Management*. New York: HarperBusiness.

Hirshberg, J. 1998. *The Creative Priority: Driving Innovative Business in the Real World*. New York: HarperBusiness.

Leonard, D.A. and W.C. Swap. 1999. *When Sparks Fly: Igniting Group Creativity*. Boston, MA: Harvard Business School Press.

Leonard-Barton, D. 1995. *Wellsprings of Knowledge: Building and Sustaining the Sources of Innovation*. Boston, MA: Harvard Business School Press.

Nonaka, I. and H. Takeuchi. 1995. *The Knowledge Creating Company: How Japanese Companies Create Dynamics of Innovation*. London: Oxford University Press.

Bibliography

Penrose, E. 1959. *The Theory of Growth of Firm*. New York: Oxford University Press.

Polanyi, M. 1967. *The Tacit Dimension*. New York: Doubleday.

Quinn, J.B., J.J. Baruch and K.A. Zien. 1997. *Innovation Explosion*. New York: The Free Press.

Senge, Peter M. 1990. *The Fifth Discipline: The Art and Practice of the Learning Organization*. New York: Doubleday.

Shukla, A. and R. Srinivasan. 2002. *Designing Knowledge Management Architecture: How to Implement Successful Knowledge Management Programmes*. New Delhi: Response Books.

Steinberg, S.H. 1974. *Five Hundred Years of Printing*. Harmondsworth: Penguin Books.

Syrett, M. and J. Lammiman. 2002. *Successful Innovation*. London: Profile Books Ltd.

Vise, D.A. 2005. *The Google Story*. London: MacMillan.

Index

About the Author

❀

Manu Parashar is CEO of *Gone to Fish*, an innovation consultancy at Bangalore. In his present profile he provides new insights and ideas to the Indian industry. Concurrently, he is also working on his doctoral degree from the Indian Institute of Management, Bangalore, in the area of social capital.

A management graduate from Indian Institute of Management, Calcutta, Manu has had nine years of corporate experience across three major companies, Godrej Sara Lee, Cadbury and Ford India Ltd. As a management thinker, he has presented papers in India as well as abroad and has been widely published in many journals.